No-Nc
Extra Class
License Study Guide

(for tests given between July 2016 and June 2020)

Dan Romanchik KB6NU

ISBN: 1530908671
ISBN-13: 978-1530908677

Version 1.0, May 2016

CONTENTS

ACKNOWLEDGMENTS

Thanks to everyone who proofread and commented on the sections I've posted on my blog, especially Frank, WA8WHP, Jim, N8NZB, and Sam, K8NOS. Your comments have really made this study guide better.

Thanks, also to Jeff, K1NSS, of Dashtoons fame, for the cover design. Jeff's covers have taken my books to the next level.

And, last but not least, thanks to all my readers. It's very rewarding for me to be able to help you all have more fun with amateur radio.

WHY YOU SHOULD GET YOUR EXTRA CLASS LICENSE

The Amateur Extra Class license is the highest class of license in the United States, and perhaps the world. Many hams—even hams that live outside the U.S.—aspire to pass the test and be awarded one.

There wasn't always an Amateur Extra Class license. The Extra Class license, as we know it today, was created as part of the 1951 license restructuring, that also created the Novice and Technician Class licenses. (In 1951, the Novice license was the "beginner's license." To get a Technician Class license, you had to pass the written exam for the General Class license.)

Although it gave an operator no additional privileges, to get an Extra Class license, one had to:

- Pass a 20 wpm code test (Generals had to pass only a 13 wpm code test).
- Pass a longer and more difficult written examination than the General Class exam.
- Have at least two years of experience as a licensed radio amateur.

Today, without the code test and the experience requirement, many hams upgrade to Extra Class as soon as they can. Some even pass the Technician Class, General Class, and the Amateur Extra Class exams in a single test session.

So, what's the attraction? Why should you upgrade to Extra?

One of the reasons that you should upgrade to Extra is that you get to use the entire 80 m, 40 m, 20 m, and 15 m bands. Portions of those bands, such as 3.6 – 3.7 MHz in the 75m band and 14.150 – 14.175 MHz in the 20m phone band, are reserved exclusively for Extra Class licensees. Extra Class operators also have exclusive privileges in the CW portions of the 80 m, 40 m, 20 m, and 15 m bands. These are the frequencies where the DX stations hang out.

Another reason to get your Extra Class license is that only Extra Class licensees can administer General Class and Extra Class license exams. General Class operators can become Volunteer Examiners (VEs), but they are only allowed to administer Technician Class exams.

Another reason you might want to get an Extra Class license is to get a fancy vanity callsign. Only Extra Class operators can apply for 1x2 or 2x1 callsigns, such as W8RP or KT8K. A short, snappy callsign can help you work more DX and improve your contest scores.

Whatever your reason, studying for the Extra Class exam will open your eyes to many aspects of the hobby that you may not be familiar with. And, as you work your way through the material, you will learn things that make you a better radio amateur and enable you to enjoy the hobby more. Based on the comments I've had from many readers, I'm convinced that this study guide will not only help you get your Extra ticket, but in the end, help you have more fun with amateur radio.

My own story

I didn't take the Extra Class test until 2006, 35 years after I got my Novice license and almost 30 years after I got my Advanced license. At first, it was the 20 wpm code test that put me off. At that point, I wasn't getting on the air enough to get my speed up to 20 wpm. Later in life, I was afraid that I'd actually fail the written test. Besides, I had a good rejoinder whenever I was asked why I didn't have an Extra Class license. I used to joke that I wanted to be the last living

Advanced Class licensee in the U.S.

After I started teaching amateur radio classes and writing these license study guides, I decided it was time to get the Extra. Besides, some of my students had already gotten their Extra Class licenses, and I found it a bit embarrassing to have "only" an Advanced ticket. So, in 2006, I decided it was time to study and take the test.

I used the ARRL study guide. It did the job, and the test was actually a little easier than I'd anticipated. Even so, I answered three questions incorrectly. I don't know that I'd have done any better if there had been a "No-Nonsense" study guide available for me to use, but my guess is that it would not have. There are just so many things that you have to memorize that you're bound to forget something.

At first, I wasn't planning to produce an Extra Class study guide. I am basically a lazy person, and I knew that writing this study guide would take a long time. The Extra Class question pool covers a lot more material than the Technician Class and General Class exams, and the material is a lot more complex, too.

In the end, though, I knew that I would do it. Every week, I'd get emails from readers asking if or when a *No-Nonsense Extra Class License Study Guide* was going to be available, and my product lineup was incomplete without it.

That was four years ago, and this is the second edition of the *No Nonsense Extra Class License Study Guide*. I sold hundreds of the first edition, and it makes me feel good that I have been able to help so many become Extras and enjoy all that amateur radio has to offer.

How to use this study guide

First, keep in mind that this is not a textbook. It's not meant to teach circuit theory or antenna theory. Instead, it's meant to put the questions on the Extra Class test in context and help you pass the test. What some readers do is to follow along with the ARRL Handbook or Google topics as they are working their way through the study guide. These sources are able to cover these topics in more depth than I can here.

As you read through the manual you will find the answers to questions **in bold**. Question designators, such as "(E5A07)" appear at the end of sentences. This is so you can refer to the questions in the question pool, if you would like to.

Periodically, you should take practice tests. Taking practice tests will allow you to take a break from studying and give you an indication of how well you're doing. You can take practice tests online at QRZ.Com, AA9PW.Com, and several other websites.

Good luck and have fun!

I hope that you find this study guide useful and that you'll upgrade to Extra. If you have any comments, questions, compliments or complaints, I want to hear from you. E-mail me at cwgeek@kb6nu.com. My goal is to continually refine this study guide and to continually make it better.

73!

Dan Romanchik KB6NU
cwgeek@kb6nu.com, Twitter: @kb6nu

E5: ELECTRICAL PRINCIPALS

E5A - Resonance and Q: characteristics of resonant circuits; series and parallel resonance; Q; half-power bandwidth; phase relationships in reactive circuits

Resonance is one of the coolest things in electronics. Resonant circuits are what makes radio, as we know it, possible.

What is resonance? Well, a circuit is said to be resonant when the inductive reactance and capacitive reactance are equal to one another. That is to say, when

$$2\pi fL = 1/(2\pi fC)$$

where L is the inductance in henries and C is the capacitance in farads.

For a given L and a given C, this happens at only one frequency:

$$f = 1/(2\pi\sqrt{(LC)})$$

This frequency is called the resonant frequency. Resonance in an electrical circuit is **the frequency at which the capacitive reactance equals the inductive reactance**. (E5A02)

Let's calculate a few resonant frequencies, using questions from the Extra question pool as examples:

The resonant frequency of a series RLC circuit if R is 22 ohms, L is 50 microhenries and C is 40 picofarads is **3.56 MHz**. (E5A14)

$$f = 1/(2\pi\sqrt{(LC)}) = 1/(6.28 \times \sqrt{(50 \times 10^{-6} \times 40 \times 10^{-12})}) =$$
$$1/(2.8 \times 10^{-7}) = 3.56\ \text{MHz}$$

Notice that it really doesn't matter what the value of the resistance is. The resonant frequency would be the same if R had been 220 ohms or 2.2 Mohms.

The resonant frequency of a parallel RLC circuit if R is 33 ohms, L is 50 microhenries and C is 10 picofarads is **7.12 MHz**. (E5A16)

$$f = 1/(2\pi\sqrt{(LC)}) = 1/(6.28 \times \sqrt{(50 \times 10^{-6} \times 10 \times 10^{-12})}) =$$
$$1/(1.4 \times 10^{-7}) = 7.12\ \text{MHz}$$

When an inductor and a capacitor are connected in series, the impedance of the series circuit at the resonant frequency is zero because the reactances are equal and opposite at that frequency. If there is a resistor in the circuit, that resistor alone contributes to the impedance. Therefore, the magnitude of the impedance of a series RLC circuit at resonance is **approximately equal to circuit resistance**. (E5A03)

The magnitude of the current at the input of a series RLC circuit is at **maximum** as the frequency goes through resonance. (E5A05) The reason for this is that neither the capacitor or inductor adds to the overall circuit impedance at the resonant frequency.

When the inductor and capacitor are connected in parallel, the reactances are again equal and opposite to one another at the resonant frequency, but because they are in parallel, the circuit is effectively an open circuit. Consequently, the magnitude of the impedance of a circuit with a resistor, an inductor and a capacitor all in parallel, at resonance, is **approximately equal to circuit resistance**. (E5A04)

Because a parallel LC circuit is effectively an open circuit at resonance, the magnitude of the current at the input of a parallel RLC circuit at resonance is at **minimum**. (E5A07) The magnitude of the circulating current within the components of a parallel LC circuit at resonance **is at a maximum**. (E5A06) **Resonance** can cause the voltage across reactances in series to be larger than the voltage applied to them. (E5A01)

6

Another consequence of the inductive and capacitive reactances canceling each other is that there is no phase shift at the resonant frequency. The phase relationship between the current through and the voltage across a series resonant circuit at resonance is that **the voltage and current are in phase.** (E5A08)

Ideally, a series LC circuit would have zero impedance at the resonant frequency, while a parallel LC circuit would have an infinite impedance at the resonant frequency. In the real world, of course, resonant circuits don't act this way. To describe how closely a circuit behaves like an ideal resonant circuit, we use the quality factor, or Q. Because the inductive reactance equals the capacitive reactance at the resonant frequency, the Q of an RLC parallel circuit is the **resistance divided by the reactance of either the inductance or capacitance** (E5A09):

$$Q = R/X_L \text{ or } R/X_C$$

The Q of an RLC series resonant circuit is the **reactance of either the inductance or capacitance divided by the resistance** (E5A10):

$$Q = X_L/R \text{ or } X_C/R$$

Basically, the higher the Q, the more a resonant circuit behaves like an ideal resonant circuit, and the higher the Q, the lower the resistive losses in a circuit. **Lower losses** can increase Q for inductors and capacitors. (E5A15) An effect of increasing Q in a resonant circuit is that **internal voltages and circulating currents increase.** (E5A13)

Q is an important parameter when designing impedance-matching circuits. The result of increasing the Q of an impedance-matching circuit is that **matching bandwidth is decreased.** (E5A17) A circuit with a lower Q will yield a wider bandwidth, but at the cost of increased losses.

A parameter of a resonant circuit that is related to Q is the half-power bandwidth. The half-power bandwidth is the bandwidth over which a series resonant circuit will pass half the power of the input signal and over which a parallel resonant circuit will reject half the power of an input signal.

We can use the Q of a circuit to calculate the half-power

bandwidth:

$BW = f/Q$

Let's look at some examples:

The half-power bandwidth of a parallel resonant circuit that has a resonant frequency of 7.1 MHz and a Q of 150 is **47.3 kHz**. (E5A11)

$BW = f/Q = 7.1 \times 10^6/150 = 47.3 \times 10^3 = 47.3$ kHz

What is the half-power bandwidth of a parallel resonant circuit that has a resonant frequency of 3.7 MHz and a Q of 118 is **31.4 kHz**. (E5A12)

$BW = f/Q = 3.5 \times 10^6/118 = 31.4 \times 10^3 = 31.4$ kHz

E5B - Time constants and phase relationships: RLC time constants; definition; time constants in RL and RC circuits; phase angle between voltage and current; phase angles of series RLC; phase angle of inductance vs susceptance; admittance and susceptance

When you put a voltage across a capacitor, current will flow into the capacitor and the voltage across the capacitor will increase until the voltage across it reaches the value of the supply voltage. This is not a linear function. By that I mean that the voltage will increase quite rapidly at first, but the rate of increase will slow as time goes on.

To see how this works, let's consider the RC time constant. The time constant of an RC circuit is equal to the resistance in the circuit times the capacitance, or simply R x C. For example, the time constant of a circuit having two 220-microfarad capacitors and two 1-megohm resistors, all in parallel is **220 seconds**. (E5B04)

The equivalent resistance of two 1 MΩ resistors in parallel is 500 kΩ. The equivalent capacitance of two 220 µF capacitors in parallel is 440 µF. The time constant is R x C = 440 x 10^{-6} x 500 x 10^3 = 220 s.

One time constant is the term for the time required for the capacitor in an RC circuit to be charged to 63.2% of the applied voltage. (E5B01) Similarly, **one time constant** is the term for the time it takes for a charged capacitor in an RC circuit to discharge to 36.8% of its initial voltage. (E5B02)

A capacitor charges to 86.5% of the applied voltage, or discharges to 13.5% of the starting voltage, after two time constants. After three time constants, a capacitor is charged up to 95% of the applied voltage or discharged to 5% of the starting voltage.

Phase relationships

In an AC circuit, with only resistors, the voltage and current are in phase. What that means is that the voltage and current change in lock step. When the voltage increases, the current increases. When the voltage decreases, the current decreases.

When there are capacitors and inductors in an AC circuit,

however, the phase relationship between the voltage and current changes. Specifically, the relationship between the current through a capacitor and the voltage across a capacitor is that the **current leads voltage by 90 degrees**. (E5B09) We could also say that the voltage lags the current by 90 degrees. See figure below.

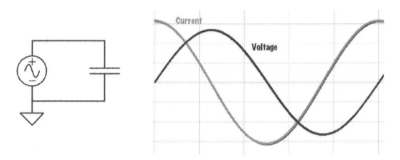

When we say that the current leads the voltage, or that the voltage lags the current, it means that the current through a capacitor increases and decreases before the voltage across a capacitor increases and decreases. We say that the current leads the voltage by 90 degrees because it starts increasing one-quarter of a cycle before the voltage starts increasing.

The relationship between the current through an inductor and the voltage across an inductor is that the **voltage leads current by 90 degrees**. (E5B10) We could also say that the current lags the voltage. See figure below.

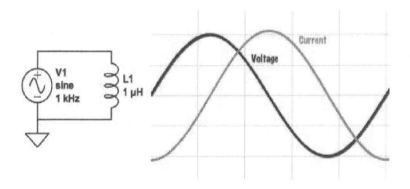

When we say that the voltage leads the current, or the current lags the voltage, it means that the voltage across an inductor increases and decreases before the current through the inductor increases and decreases. We say that the voltage leads the current by 90 degrees because it starts increasing one-quarter of a cycle before the current starts increasing.

When there are resistors as well as a capacitor or inductor or both in a circuit, the relationship is a little more complicated. Let's look at what happens in the series RLC circuit shown below.

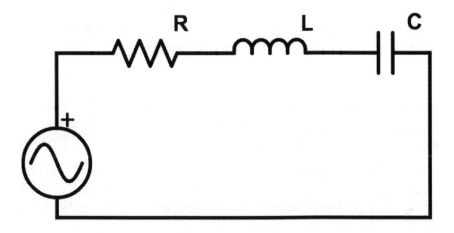

In this circuit, there is resistance, capacitive reactance, and inductive reactance. The reactances subtract from one another. If the capacitive reactance is greater than the inductive reactance, the net reactance will be capacitive. If the inductive reactance is greater than the capacitive reactance, the net reactance will be inductive.

The resistance and the reactance add to one another, but they add vectorially. The reason for this is that the reactance will be 90 degrees out of phase with the resistance. This is shown in the figure below.

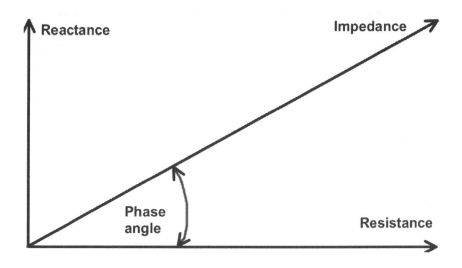

The magnitude of the impedance, Z, will be equal to $\sqrt{(R^2 + X^2)}$ and the tangent of the phase angle will be equal to X/R. Let's see how this works in several examples.

If X_C is 500 ohms, R is 1 kilohm, and X_L is 250 ohms, the phase angle between the voltage across and the current through the series RLC circuit is **14.0 degrees with the voltage lagging the current**. (E5B07) Here's how to calculate that:

$X = X_C - X_L = 250\ \Omega$ (capacitive)

phase angle $= \tan^{-1}(250/1000) = 14$ degrees.

and because the reactance is capacitive, the voltage will lag the current.

If X_C is 100 ohms, R is 100 ohms, and X_L is 75 ohms, the phase angle between the voltage across and the current through the series RLC circuit is **14 degrees with the voltage lagging the current**. (E5B08) Here's the calculation:

$X = X_C - X_L = 25\ \Omega$ (capacitive)

phase angle $= \tan^{-1}(25/100) = 14$ degrees.

and because the reactance is capacitive, the voltage lags the current.

If X_C is 25 ohms, R is 100 ohms, and X_L is 50 ohms, the phase angle between the voltage across and the current through the series RLC circuit is **14 degrees with the voltage leading the current**. (E5B11) Here's the calculation:

$X = X_L - X_C = 25\ \Omega$ (inductive)

phase angle = $\tan^{-1}(25/100) = 14$ degrees.

and because the reactance is inductive, the voltage leads the current.

Susceptance and admittance

While we most often work with reactances and impedances in amateur radio, in some cases, it's more advantageous to work with susceptance and admittance.

Susceptance is **the inverse of reactance**. (E5B06) The unit of susceptance is the siemens (S). **B** is the letter is commonly used to represent susceptance. (E5B13) In mathematical terms,

$B = 1/X$

When the magnitude of a reactance is converted to a susceptance, **the magnitude of the susceptance is the reciprocal of the magnitude of the reactance**. (E5B05) When the phase angle of a reactance is converted to a susceptance, **the sign is reversed**. (E5B03)

Admittance is **the inverse of impedance**. (E5B12) The unit of admittance is the siemens, and like impedance, is a complex quantity.

E5C - Impedance plots and coordinate systems: plotting impedances in polar coordinates; rectangular coordinates

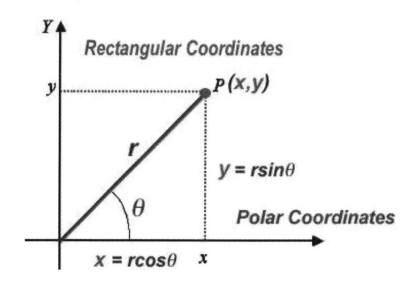

Most often when we plot values on a graph, we use the rectangular, or Cartesian, coordinate system. The two numbers that are used to define a point on a graph using rectangular coordinates are **the coordinate values along the horizontal and vertical axes**. (E5C11) In the graph above, point P is at x,y.

Rectangular coordinates is the coordinate system often used to display the resistive, inductive, and/or capacitive reactance components of an impedance. (E5C13) When using rectangular coordinates to graph the impedance of a circuit, the horizontal axis represents the **resistive component**. (E5C09) When using rectangular coordinates to graph the impedance of a circuit, the vertical axis represents the **reactive component**. (E5C10)

In rectangular notation, $-jX$ represents a capacitive reactance. (E5C01) The impedance 50–j25 represents **50 ohms resistance in series with 25 ohms capacitive reactance**. (E5C06) If the impedance was 50 + j25, then the circuit would have 50 ohms resistance in series with 25 ohm of inductive reactance because +jX represents an inductive reactance.

To figure out the impedance of a circuit, you first plot the inductive reactance on the positive y-axis and the capacitive reactance on the negative y-axis. The net reactance, X, will be the sum of the two reactances. After you've computed the net reactance, you plot the resistance on the x-axis and compute the magnitude of the impedance, shown by r in the graph above. If you consider that r is the third side of a right triangle made up of the sides r, x, and y, r is equal to the square root of x^2 and y^2.

If you plot the impedance of a circuit using the rectangular coordinate system and find the impedance point falls on the right side of the graph on the horizontal axis, you know that the circuit impedance **is equivalent to a pure resistance**. (E5C12)

When thinking about how capacitive reactances, inductive reactances, and resistance combine, it's useful to think in terms of polar coordinates. **Polar coordinates** is the coordinate system often used to display the phase angle of a circuit containing resistance, inductive and/or capacitive reactance. (E5C08) In a polar-coordinate system, each point on the graph has two values, a magnitude (shown by r in the figure above) and an angle (shown by θ in the figure above).

In polar coordinates, impedances are described **by phase angle and amplitude**. (E5C02) These kinds of quantities are sometimes called vectors. A vector is **a quantity with both magnitude and an angular component**. (E5C07)

In polar coordinates, **a positive phase angle** represents an inductive reactance. (E5C03) In polar coordinates, **a negative phase angle** represents a capacitive reactance. (E5C04) **Phasor diagram** is the name of the diagram used to show the phase relationship between impedances and resistances at a given frequency. (E5C05)

Figure E5-2

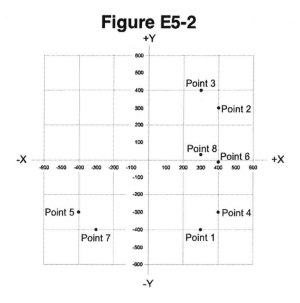

Now, let's take a look at some actual circuits.

On Figure E5-2, the point that best represents the impedance of a series circuit consisting of a 400 ohm resistor and a 38 picofarad capacitor at 14 MHz is **Point 4**. (E5C14) Right off the bat, we know that the only choices are really Points 2, 4, and 6 because the resistance is 400 ohms. Next, we calculate the capacitive reactance:

$$X_C = 1/2\pi fC = 1/(2 \times 3.14 \times 14 \times 10^6 \times 38 \times 10^{-12}) \approx 300 \text{ ohms}$$

Because the reactance is capacitive, it's plotted as a negative value.

On Figure E5-2, the point that best represents the impedance of a series circuit consisting of a 300 ohm resistor and an 18 microhenry inductor at 3.505 MHz is **Point 3**. (E5C15) The resistance is 300 ohms and the reactance is:

$$X_L = 2\pi fL = 2 \times 3.14 \times 3.505 \times 10^6 \times 18 \times 10^{-6}) \approx 400 \text{ ohms}$$

And, since the reactance is inductive, it's plotted as a postive value.

On Figure E5-2, the point that best represents the impedance of a series circuit consisting of a 300 ohm resistor and a 19 picofarad capacitor at 21.200 MHz is **Point 1**. (E5C16) The resistance is 300 ohms, and the reactance is:

$X_C = 1/2\pi fC = 1/(2 \times 3.14 \times 21.2 \times 10^6 \times 19 \times 10^{-12}) \approx 400$ ohms

Because the reactance is capacitive, it's plotted as a negative value.

On Figure E5-2, the point that best represents the impedance of a series circuit consisting of a 300-ohm resistor, a 0.64-microhenry inductor and an 85-picofarad capacitor at 29.400 MHz is **Point 8**. (E5C17) This problem is a little tougher because it has both capacitive and inductive reactance.

$X_C = 1/2\pi fC = 1/(2 \times 3.14 \times 29.4 \times 10^6 \times 85 \times 10^{-12}) \approx 63.7$ ohms

$X_L = 2\pi fL = 2 \times 3.14 \times 29.4 \times 10^6 \times 0.64 \times 10^{-6}) \approx 118.2$ ohms

$X = X_L - X_C = 118.2 - 63.7 = 54.5$ ohms

Because the net reactance is inductive, it is plotted as a positive value, and because the resistance is 300 ohms, the answer is Point 8.

E5D - AC and RF energy in real circuits: skin effect; electrostatic and electromagnetic fields; reactive power; power factor; electrical length of conductors at UHF and microwave frequencies

In AC circuits–and RF circuits are just a type of AC circuit–capacitors and inductors store and release energy as the voltages and currents change. Because of this, calculating power and energy in an AC circuit is not as straightforward as it is for DC circuits.

Capacitors store electrical energy in an electrostatic field. During the positive portion of an AC cycle, the capacitor stores energy in its electrostatic field, but during the negative portion of the cycle, it returns that energy to the circuit.

Inductors store electrical energy in a magnetic field. The current through the inductor creates the magnetic field. **The amount of current** determines the strength of a magnetic field around a conductor. (E5D07) The direction of the magnetic field oriented about a conductor in relation to the direction of electron flow runs **in a direction determined by the left-hand rule**. (E5D06)

A similar thing happens to the magnetic field created by the current flow through an inductor that happens to the electrostatic field in a capacitor. When the current flows in one direction, a magnetic field is created. When the current changes direction, the energy stored in that magnetic field gets returned to the circuit.

The type of energy that is stored in an electromagnetic or electrostatic field is **potential energy** (E5D08)

Reactive power

When talking about the power consumed by AC circuits, an important concept is reactive power. Reactive power is **wattless, nonproductive power**. (E5D14)

As noted above, during some portions of an AC cycle, inductors and capacitors will draw current and store energy, but during other portions of the cycle, it will return that energy to the circuit. So, what happens to reactive power in an AC circuit that has both ideal inductors and ideal capacitors is that **it is repeatedly exchanged** between the associated magnetic and electric fields, but is not dissipated. (E5D09) In other words, the net power dissipation is zero.

Of course, very few circuits contain only capacitors and inductors. In AC circuits where there is a resistance, that resistance will dissipate real power. For example, in a circuit consisting of a 100 ohm resistor in series with a 100 ohm inductive reactance drawing 1 ampere, the power consumed is **100 Watts.** (E5D13) (P = I^2 × R = $1A^2$ × 100 ohms = 100 W.)

In an AC circuit with inductors and capacitors, the voltage is out of phase with the current. You determine the true power of an AC circuit where the voltage and current are out of phase **by multiplying the apparent power times the power factor.** (E5D10) For example, if a circuit has a power factor of 0.71 and the apparent power is 500 VA, the watts consumed is **355 W.** (E5D18)

The power factor, or PF, is the cosine of the phase angle between the voltage and current. For example, if an R-L circuit has a 60 degree phase angle between the voltage and the current, the power factor is the cosine of 60 degrees, or **0.5** (E5D11) The power factor of an R-L circuit having a 45 degree phase angle between the voltage and the current is the cosine of 45 degrees, or **0.707.** (E5D15) The power factor of an RL circuit having a 30 degree phase angle between the voltage and the current is the cosine of 30 degrees, or **0.866.** (E5D16)

Let's look at a few examples:

- If a circuit has a power factor of 0.2, and the input is 100 VAC at 4 amperes, the watts consumed is V × I × PF = 100 V × 4 A × 0.2 = **80 watts.** (E5D12)
- If a circuit has a power factor of 0.6 and the input is 200 V AC at 5 amperes, the watts consumed is V × I × PF = 200 VAC × 5 A × 0.6 = **600 watts.** (E5D17)

The behavior of conductors at high frequencies

At RF frequencies, the current in a conductor tends to flow near the surface of that conductor. This phenomenon is called the skin effect. The result of skin effect is that **as frequency increases, RF current**

flows in a thinner layer of the conductor, closer to the surface. (E5D01)

At VHF, UHF, and microwave frequencies, the inductance of conductors must be taken into account. The reason for this is that inductive reactance increases with frequency, and at high frequencies, this reactance is no longer negligible. **Inductance** is a parasitic characteristic that increases with conductor length. (E5D05) It is, therefore, important to keep lead lengths short for components used in circuits for VHF and above **to avoid unwanted inductive reactance.** (E5D02)

Another phenomenon that occurs at high frequencies is that printed circuit board traces begin to act like transmission lines instead of just simple conductors. To properly connect components and circuits, printed circuit board designers carefully lay out the traces so that they have a constant impedance. **Microstrips** are precision printed circuit leads above a ground plane that provide constant impedance interconnects at microwave frequencies. (E5D03)

At microwave frequencies, it is also import to keep connections as short as possible. Short connections are necessary at microwave frequencies **to reduce phase shift along the connection.** (E5D04)

E6: CIRCUIT COMPONENTS

E6A - Semiconductor materials and devices: semiconductor materials; germanium, silicon, P-type, N-type; transistor types: NPN, PNP, junction, field-effect transistors: enhancement mode; depletion mode; MOS; CMOS; N-channel; P-channel

While transistor theory is outside the scope of this study guide, I will attempt to at least give you a basic understanding of how transistors are put together and how they work. For more information, take a look at these two links:

- How Semiconductors Work
  (http://www.howstuffworks.com/diode.htm)
- P-type and N-type silicon
  (http://www.energyresearch.nl/energieopties/zonnecellen/acht
  ergrond/techniek/p-en-n-type-silicium/)

Most transistors we use in amateur radio are made of silicon. Silicon is a semiconductor. That is to say, it's neither a conductor with a very low resistance, like copper, or an insulator with a very high resistance, like plastic or glass.

You can manipulate the electrical characteristics of silicon by adding slight amounts of impurities to a pure silicon crystal. When transistor manufacturers add an impurity that adds free electrons to the silicon crystal, it creates a crystal with a negative charge. We call that type of silicon N-type silicon. **N-type** is a semiconductor material that contains excess free electrons. (E6A02) In N-type semiconductor material, the majority charge carriers are the **free electrons**. (E6A16)

When you add other types of impurities to a pure silicon crystal, you can create a crystal with a positive charge. We call this type of material P-type semiconductor material. The majority charge carriers in P-type semiconductor material are called holes. **P-type** is the type of semiconductor material that contains an excess of holes in the outer shell of electrons. (E6A15)

You can think of holes as spots in the crystal that accept free electrons. Because of that, the name given to an impurity atom that adds holes to a semiconductor crystal structure is call an **acceptor impurity**. (E6A04)

Silicon isn't the only semiconductor material used to make transistors. **At microwave frequencies**, gallium arsenide is used as a semiconductor material in preference to germanium or silicon. (E6A01)

Semiconductor diodes

Diodes are the simplest semiconductor devices. A PN junction diode is formed when you join a bit of P-type material to a bit of N-type material. When you join the two materials, some electrons from the N-type material migrate over to the P-type material and fill holes there. As a result, holes form in the N-type material. This migration of charge forms what is called the depletion region at the PN junction, and an electric field forms across this region. The electric field generates a voltage across the junction.

The most important characteristic of a PN junction diode is that it only allows current to flow when it is forward-biased, that is to say when the voltage applied to the P-type material is more positive than the voltage applied to the N-type material. When a PN junction diode is reversed biased—that is when the voltage applied to the P-type material is more negative than the voltage applied to the N-type material—the diode will not conduct current. A PN-junction diode does not conduct current when reverse biased because **holes in P-type material and electrons in the N-type material are separated by the applied voltage, widening the depletion region**. (E6A03) This makes it impossible for current to flow through the region

Bipolar junction transistors

Perhaps the most popular type of transistor is the bipolar junction transistor (BJT). Bipolar junction transistors have three terminals, called the emitter, base, and collector. In an NPN transistor, the emitter and collector are N-type material and the base is P-type material. In a PNP transistor, the emitter and collector are P-type, while the base is N-type. The base is sandwiched between the collector and emitter, so there is a diode junction between the base and the collector and the base and emitter. The schematic symbols for these transistors are shown below.

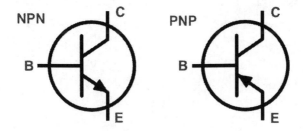

B=base, C=collector, E=emitter

When the base-emitter diode is forward-biased, a current, called the base current will flow. A **base-to-emitter voltage of approximately 0.6 to 0.7 volts** indicates that a silicon NPN junction transistor is biased on. (E6A07)

When a silicon NPN junction transistor is biased on, a small base current will flow, and this base current will cause a much larger current to flow from the collector through the base to the emitter. The amount of base current controls how much collector current flows. This is how transistors amplify signals.

The change in collector current with respect to base current is the beta of a bipolar junction transistor. (E6A06) This is also sometimes called the hfe, or current gain, of a transistor.

A related specification is the alpha of a transistor. **The change of collector current with respect to emitter current** is the alpha of a bipolar junction transistor. (E6A05)

Another important characteristic of a bipolar transistor is the alpha cutoff frequency. This is a measure of how high in frequency a transistor will operate. **Alpha cutoff frequency** is the frequency at which the grounded-base current gain of a transistor has decreased to 0.7 of the gain obtainable at 1 kHz. (E6A08)

Field effect transistors

A field-effect transistor (FET) is a device that uses an electric field to control current flow through the device. Like the bipolar transistor, a FET normally has three terminals. The names of the three terminals of a field-effect transistor are **gate, drain, source**. (E6A17)

FETs are normally made with a technology called Complementary Metal-Oxide Semiconductor, or CMOS. The initials CMOS stand for **Complementary Metal-Oxide Semiconductor**. (E6A13) FETs made with CMOS technology are sometimes call MOSFETs.

In Figure E6-2 (below), schematic symbol **1** is the symbol for a P-channel junction FET. (E6A11) In Figure E6-2 (below), schematic symbol **4** is the symbol for an N-channel dual-gate MOSFET. (E6A10)

Figure E6-2

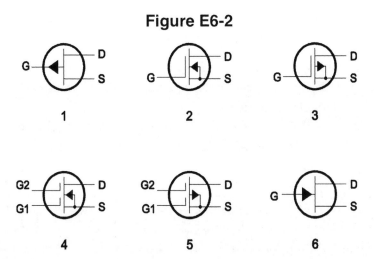

One characteristic of MOSFETs is that they have a high input impedance. This makes them more attractive than bipolar transistors in many test equipment applications. How does DC input impedance at the gate of a field-effect transistor compare with the DC input impedance of a bipolar transistor? **An FET has high input impedance; a bipolar transistor has low input impedance.** (E6A14)

One disadvantage of using MOSFETs is that they are very sensitive to electrostatic discharge (ESD). Sometimes, they are damaged by static discharges so low that you never even see the spark or feel the shock. **To reduce the chance of the gate insulation being punctured by static discharges or excessive voltages** many MOSFET devices have internally connected Zener diodes on the gates. (E6A12)

Most FETs are enhancement-mode devices. When using an enhancement-mode FET, you must apply a voltage to the gate to get current to flow from source to drain. Some FETs are, however, depletion mode devices. A depletion-mode FET is **an FET that exhibits a current flow between source and drain when no gate voltage is applied.** (E6A09)

E6B - Diodes

Diodes have two terminals and conduct current in only one direction, from the cathode to the anode. By manipulating the characteristics of the semiconductor material, manufacturers can make diodes useful in a wide variety of applications.

Take, for example, the Zener diode. The most useful characteristic of a Zener diode is **a constant voltage drop under conditions of varying current**. (E6B01) This makes it useful in voltage regulator circuits.

Another example is the varactor diode. The **varactor diode** is a semiconductor device designed for use as a voltage-controlled capacitor. (E6B04) Varactor diodes are often used in tuning circuits.

A PIN diode is a semiconductor device that operates as a variable resistor at RF and microwave frequencies. One common use for PIN diodes is **as an RF switch**. (E6B12) The characteristic of a PIN diode that makes it useful as an RF switch or attenuator is **a large region of intrinsic material**. (E6B05) **The forward DC bias current** is used to control the attenuation of RF signals by a PIN diode. (E6B11)

Two types of diodes used in RF circuits are the tunnel diode and hot-carrier diode. The **tunnel** diode is a special type of diode that is capable of both amplification and oscillation. (E6B03) Tunnel diodes are capable of operating well into the microwave region. A hot-carrier diode is commonly used **as a VHF / UHF mixer or detector**. (E6B06)

Metal-semiconductor junction is a term that describes a type of semiconductor diode. (E6B08) A Schottky diode is an example of a metal-semiconductor diode. An important characteristic of a Schottky diode as compared to an ordinary silicon diode when used as a power supply rectifier is that it has **less forward voltage drop**. (E6B02) This characteristic also makes them useful in digital logic circuits. The lower forward voltage drop allows the digital ICs to switch faster.

Another type of diode is the point-contact diode. A common use for point-contact diodes is **as an RF detector**. (E6B09)

In Figure E6-3 (below), **5** is the schematic symbol for a light-emitting diode. (E6B10) **Forward bias** is required for an LED to emit light. (E6B13)

Figure E6-3

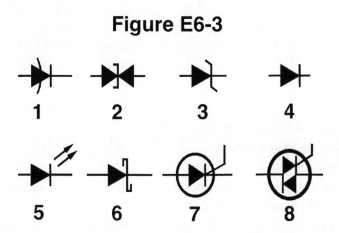

No matter what kind of diode you are using, it's very important to not exceed the forward current specification. Doing so, will cause it to fail. **Excessive junction temperature** is the failure mechanism when a junction diode fails due to excessive current. (E6B07)

E6C - Digital ICs: Families of digital ICs; gates; Programmable Logic Devices (PLDs)

Integrated circuits (ICs) are now an integral part (pun intended) of amateur radio electronics. There are several different technologies used to manufacture ICs including transistor-transistor logic, or TTL; complementary metal-oxide semiconductor, or CMOS; and BiCMOS, which uses a combination of bipolar and CMOS transistors.

CMOS is arguably the most common type of digital IC. An advantage of CMOS logic devices over TTL devices is that the have **lower power consumption**. (E6C05) CMOS digital integrated circuits also have high immunity to noise on the input signal or power supply because **the input switching threshold is about one-half the power supply voltage**. (E6C06)

BiCMOS logic is **an integrated circuit logic family using both bipolar and CMOS transistors**. (E6C12) An advantage of BiCMOS logic is that **it has the high input impedance of CMOS and the low output impedance of bipolar transistors**. (E6C13)

Tri-state logic devices are **logic devices with 0, 1, and high impedance output states**. (E6C03) These devices can be made with either TTL or CMOS technology. The primary advantage of tri-state logic is the **ability to connect many device outputs to a common bus**. (EC604) When a device's outputs are in the high-impedance state, they act as if they are disconnected.

Figure E6-5

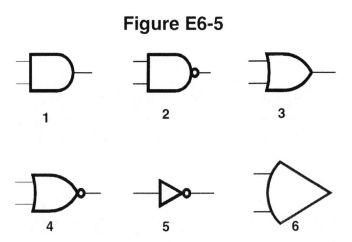

When working with digital ICs, it is important to recognize the various symbols for the different types of logic gates. In Figure E6-5, **2** is the schematic symbol for a NAND gate. (E6C08) In Figure E6-5, **4** is the schematic symbol for a NOR gate. (E6C10) In Figure E6-5, **5** is the schematic symbol for the NOT operation (inverter). (E6C11)

When designing circuits with digital ICs, you may not use all of the inputs of the gates in that IC. To set that input to a digital 1 or 0, you might use a pull-up resistor or a pull-down resistor. A pull-up or pull-down resistor is best described as **a resistor connected to the positive or negative supply line used to establish a voltage when an input or output is an open circuit**. (E6C07) Pull-up resistors are also often used on the output of a digital circuit to prevent that output from floating.

A particular type of IC is called a comparator. Comparators compare an input voltage to a threshold voltage, and when the level of a comparator's input signal crosses the threshold is **the comparator changes its output state**. (E6C02)

Comparators have a property called hysteresis. Basically, what this means is that the threshold voltage is lower when the input voltage is decreasing than the threshold voltage when the input voltage is increasing. The function of hysteresis in a comparator is **to prevent input noise from causing unstable output signals**. (E6C01) If the threshold voltage was the same for both increasing and decreasing input voltages, and the input voltage was right at the threshold voltage, then noise could cause that input voltage to go above and below the threshold randomly. If the comparator input did not have hysteresis, then its output would switch randomly.

Many modern electronic devices now use programmable logic devices instead of cobbling together a digital circuit with a collection of ICs with simple gates. A Programmable Logic Device (PLD) is **a programmable collection of logic gates and circuits in a single integrated circuit**. (E6C09). Programmable logic devices can have thousands or even millions of gates in a single IC. To design digital circuits with PLDs, designers use computer-aided design software to connect and configure the logic gates.

A programmable gate array is a particular type of programmable logic device. The primary advantage of using a Programmable Gate Array (PGA) in a logic circuit is that **complex logic functions can be created in a single integrated circuit**. (E6C14)

E6D - Toroidal and solenoidal Inductors: permeability, core material, selecting, winding; transformers; piezoelectric devices

Solenoidal and toroidal inductors are both used in amateur radio equipment. A solenoidal inductor is a coil of wire wound around a cylindrical core, while a toroidal inductor is a coil of wire wound around a circular or toroidal core. Solenoidal inductors often have just an air core, while toroidal inductors are wound around a ferrite or powdered-iron core.

A primary advantage of using a toroidal core instead of a solenoidal core in an inductor is that **toroidal cores confine most of the magnetic field within the core material**. (E6D10) The usable frequency range of inductors that use toroidal cores, assuming a correct selection of core material for the frequency being used, is **from less than 20 Hz to approximately 300 MHz.** (E6D07)

An important characteristic of a toroid core is its permeability. **Permeability** is the core material property that determines the inductance of a toroidal inductor. (E6D06)

One important reason for using powdered-iron toroids rather than ferrite toroids in an inductor is that **powdered-iron toroids generally maintain their characteristics at higher currents**. (E6D08) One reason for using ferrite toroids rather than powdered-iron toroids in an inductor is that **ferrite toroids generally require fewer turns to produce a given inductance value**. (E6D05) **Ferrite beads** are commonly used as VHF and UHF parasitic suppressors at the input and output terminals of transistorized HF amplifiers. (E6D09)

To calculate the inductance of a ferrite-core toroid, we need the inductance index of the core material. The formula that we use to calculate the inductance of a ferrite-core toroid inductor is:

$$L = A_L \times N^2 / 1{,}000{,}000$$

where L = inductance in microhenries, A_L = inductance index in μH per 1000 turns, and N = number of turns

We can solve for N to get the following formula:

$$N = 1000 \times \sqrt{(L/A_L)}$$

Using that equation, we see that **43 turns** will be required to produce a 1-mH inductor using a ferrite toroidal core that has an inductance index (A L) value of 523 millihenries/1000 turns. (E6D11)

$$N = 1000 \times \sqrt{(1/523)} = 1000 \times .0437 = 43.7 \text{ turns}$$

The formula for calculating the inductance of a powdered-iron core toroid inductor is:

$$L = A_L \times N^2 / 10,000$$

where L = inductance in microhenries, A_L = inductance index in µH per 1000 turns, and N = number of turns. We can solve for N to get the following formula:

$$N = 100 \times \sqrt{(L/A_L)}$$

Using that equation, **35 turns** turns will be required to produce a 5-microhenry inductor using a powdered-iron toroidal core that has an inductance index (A L) value of 40 microhenries/100 turns. (E6D01)

$$N = 1000 \times \sqrt{(5/40)} = 100 \times .353 = 35.3 \text{ turns}$$

When designing circuits with ferrite-core inductors, you have to be careful not to saturate the core. The definition of saturation in a ferrite core inductor is that **the ability of the inductor's core to store magnetic energy has been exceeded**. (E6D12)

One problem that may occur in a circuit with inductors is self-resonance. The primary cause of inductor self-resonance is **inter-turn capacitance**. (E6D13) At some frequency, also called the "self-resonant frequency," this capacitance forms a parallel resonant circuit with the inductor.

Variable inductors are made by inserting a slug into an air-core inductor. By varying the position of the slug, you vary the inductance. **Ferrite and brass** are materials commonly used as a slug core in a variable inductor. (E6D04) **Brass** is the type of slug material decreases inductance when inserted into a coil. (E6D14)

Transformers

A transformer consists of two inductors that are closely coupled.

Connecting an AC voltage across one of the inductors, called the primary winding, causes a current to flow in the primary, which then generates a magnetic field. As the lines of this field cross the turns of the secondary winding, it induces a current to flow in the secondary, and the voltage across the secondary is equal to the voltage across the primary winding times the number of turns in the secondary winding divided by the number of turns in the primary winding. The current in the primary winding of a transformer is called the **magnetizing current** if no load is attached to the secondary. (E6D15)

Transformers are often used to match the output impedance of one circuit to the input impedance of another. In this application, it's important not to saturate the core of the transformer. The core saturation of a conventional impedance matching transformer should be avoided because **harmonics and distortion could result**. (E6D17)

In some applications, a transformer's secondary winding may be subjected to voltage spikes. In these applications, the designer may connect a capacitor to absorb the energy in that voltage spike to prevent damage to the transformer. The common name for a capacitor connected across a transformer secondary that is used to absorb transient voltage spikes is **snubber capacitor**. (E6D16)

Piezoelectric devices

Piezoelectric crystals are used in several amateur radio applications. They are called piezoelectric crystals because they rely on the piezoelectric effect, which is the **physical deformation of a crystal by the application of a voltage**. (E6D03) The equivalent circuit of a quartz crystal is a **motional capacitance, motional inductance, and loss resistance in series, all in parallel with a shunt capacitor representing electrode and stray capacitance**. (E6D02)

E6E Analog ICs: MMICs, CCDs, device packages

Monolithic microwave integrated circuits, or MMICs, are ICs that are made to perform various functions at high frequencies. **Gallium nitride** is a material that is likely to provide the highest frequency of operation when used in MMICs. (E6E03) The characteristics of the MMIC that make it a popular choice for VHF through microwave circuits are **controlled gain, low noise figure, and constant input and output impedance over the specified frequency range**. (E6E06)

VHF and UHF preamplifiers are devices that might use an MMIC. A low-noise UHF preamplifier might have a typical noise figure value of **2 dB**. (E6E05) **50 ohms** is the most common input and output impedance of circuits that use MMICs. (E6E04)

To achieve these specifications, great care is taken in building and using circuits that use MMICs. For example, **microstrip construction** is typically used to construct a MMIC-based microwave amplifier. (E6E07), and the power-supply voltage is normally furnished to the most common type of monolithic microwave integrated circuit (MMIC) **through a resistor and/or RF choke connected to the amplifier output lead**. (E6E08)

Another consideration for an amplifier is heat dissipation. **Better dissipation of heat** are why high-power RF amplifier ICs and transistors sometimes mounted in ceramic packages. (E6E12)

Charge-coupled devices

Charge-coupled devices are another type of analog IC. They transform images into electrical signals. A charge-coupled device (CCD) **samples an analog signal and passes it in stages from the input to the output**. (E6E01)

Device packages

Integrated circuits come in many different types of packages. One of the most common packages for an integrated circuit is the dual-inline package, or DIP. One characteristic of DIP packaging used for integrated circuits is **a total of two rows of connecting pins placed on opposite sides of the package (Dual In-line Package)**. (E6E11)

A **DIP** device package is a through-hole type. (E6E02) This means that the leads on a DIP package are inserted into holes on a printed circuit board (PCB) that extend through the board.

For a variety of reasons, electronics companies are moving away from ICs in dual inline packages and moving towards surface-mount packages. **Surface mount** is the packaging technique in which leadless components are soldered directly to circuit boards. (E6E10)

The reason for this is that surface mount packages do not have long leads like the leads on DIPs, so the lead inductance is very low or non-existent. This means that ICs in surface-mount packages can be used at higher frequencies and that their RF behavior is more predictable. **Surface mount** is the component package type that would be most suitable for use at frequencies above the HF range. (E6E09).

E6F: Optical components: photoconductive principles and effects, photovoltaic systems, optical couplers, optical sensors, and optoisolators; LCDs

Some components make use of the photovoltaic effect. The photovoltaic effect is **the conversion of light to electrical energy**. (E6F04) In a photovoltaic cell, **electrons** absorb the energy from light falling on a photovoltaic cell. (E6F12) The electrons then become free electrons.

The most common type of photovoltaic cell used for electrical power generation is **silicon**. (E6F10) The approximate open-circuit voltage produced by a fully-illuminated silicon photovoltaic cell is **0.5 V**. (E6F11) The efficiency of a photovoltaic cell is **the relative fraction of light that is converted to current**. (E6F09)

Photoconductivity is a similar phenomenon. Photoconductivity is **the increased conductivity of an illuminated semiconductor**. (E6F01) The conductivity of a photoconductive material **increases** when light shines on it. (E6F02) **A crystalline semiconductor** is the material that is affected the most by photoconductivity. (E6F06)

A device that uses the phenomenon of photoconductivity is the optoisolator. The most common configuration of an optoisolator or optocoupler is **an LED and a phototransistor**. (E6F03) Optoisolators are often used in conjunction with solid state circuits when switching 120 VAC because **optoisolators provide a very high degree of electrical isolation between a control circuit and the circuit being switched**. (E6F08)

A similar device is the solid-state relay. A solid state relay is **a device that uses semiconductor devices to implement the functions of an electromechanical relay**. (E6F07)

Optical shaft encoders are another device that rely on photoconductivity. An optical shaft encoder is **a device which detects rotation of a control by interrupting a light source with a patterned wheel**. (E6F05) Optical shaft encoders are used to detect when an operator turns a knob on an amateur radio transceiver.

Liquid crystal displays

A liquid crystal display (LCD) is **a display utilizing a crystalline liquid and polarizing filters which becomes opaque when voltage is applied.** (E6F13) One thing that is true of LCD displays is that **they may be hard to view through polarized lenses.** (E6F14)

E7: PRACTICAL CIRCUITS

E7A - Digital circuits: digital circuit principles and logic circuits: classes of logic elements; positive and negative logic; frequency dividers; truth tables

Digital circuits are used for a variety of functions in modern amateur radio equipment. Unlike analog circuits, the output voltage of an ideal digital circuit can only be one of two values. One of these voltages—normally a positive voltage—represents a digital 1. The other value—normally near 0 V—represents a digital 0.

This type of logic is called positive logic. **Positive Logic** is the name for logic which defines a logic "1" as a high voltage. (E7A11) The logic may be reversed, though. That is to say that a high voltage may represent a logic 0. **Negative logic** is the name for logic which defines a logic "0" as a high voltage. (E7A12)

The microcomputers that control today's transceivers are very complex digital circuits. These complex digital circuits are made by combining many smaller building blocks called logic gates. These gates perform basic digital logic functions.

One of the most basic digital circuits in the NAND gate. The logical operation that a NAND gate performs is that **it produces a logic "0" at its output only when all inputs are logic "1."** (E7A07)

This logical operation can be described by a truth table. A truth table is **a list of inputs and corresponding outputs for a digital device**. (E7A10) Table E7-1 shows a truth table that describes the operation of a two-input NAND gate. A and B are the two inputs; Q is the output.

2-INPUT NAND		
A	B	Q
0	0	1
0	1	1
1	0	1
1	1	0

Table E7-1

Other types of gates perform different logical functions. The logical operation that a NOR gate performs is that **it produces a logic "0" at its output if any or all inputs are logic "1."** (E7A08) Table E7-2 shows a truth table that describes the logical operation of a NOR gate.

2-INPUT NOR		
A	B	Q
0	0	1
0	1	0
1	0	0
1	1	0

Table E7-2

The logical operation that is performed by a two-input exclusive NOR gate is that **it produces a logic "0" at its output if any single input is a logic "1."** (E7A09) Table E7-3 shows a truth table that describes the logical operation of an XNOR gate.

2-INPUT XNOR		
A	B	Q
0	0	1
0	1	0
1	0	0
1	1	1

Table E7-3

Flip-flops are circuits that are made from combinations of logic gates. By "latching" the state of an input at a particular time, a flip-flop can be said to have memory. A D flip-flop, and its truth table is shown in the figure below.

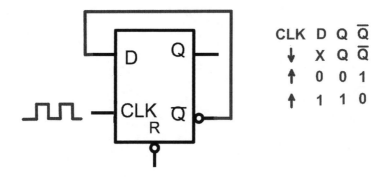

D flip-flop and truth table.

As shown, the output changes only on the rising edge of the clock (CLK) signal. That is to say, when the signal goes from 0 to 1. If D = 1, Q = 1. If D = 0, then Q = 0. The other output, denoted by a bar over the Q, is the inverse of Q.

When a D flip-flop is connected as shown in the figure—with the inverted output connected to the D input—**a flip-flop** can divide the frequency of a pulse train by 2. (E7A03) You can connect the Q output to a second flip-flop to divide the frequency even further. Consequently, **2** flip-flops are required to divide a signal frequency by 4. (E7A04)

By connecting a number of flip-flops together, and resetting the circuit once ten pulses have been input, you can build a decade counter. The function of a decade counter digital IC is to **produce one output pulse for every ten input pulses**. (E7A02)

A flip-flop is a bistable circuit. (E7A01) That means its output is stable in either state. A monostable circuit is one that is stable in one state, but not the other. One characteristic of a monostable multivibrator is that **it switches momentarily to the opposite binary state and then returns, after a set time, to its original state**. (E7A06) A trigger pulse causes the monostable vibrator to switch to the unstable state, and it stays in that state for a set period, no matter how long the trigger pulse. An **astable multivibrator** is a circuit that continuously alternates between two states without an external clock. (E7A05) In other words, it is an oscillator.

E7B - Amplifiers class of operation; vacuum tube and solid-state circuits; distortion and intermodulation; spurious and parasitic suppression; microwave amplifiers; switching-type amplifiers

There are several classes of amplifiers, based on their mode of operation. In a class A amplifier, the transistor is always conducting current. That means that the bias of a Class A common emitter amplifier would normally be set **approximately half-way between saturation and cutoff** on the load line. (E7B04)

In a class B amplifier, there are normally two transistors operating in a "push-pull" configuration. One transistor turns on during the positive half of a cycle, while the other turns on during the negative half. One advantage of using push-pull amplifiers is that **push-pull** amplifiers reduce or eliminate even-order harmonics. (E7B06)

A Class AB amplifier operates over **more than 180 degrees but less than 360 degrees** of a signal cycle. (E7B01) Class B and Class AB amplifiers are more efficient than Class A amplifiers.

Class C amplifiers conduct over less than 180 degrees of the input signal. This type of operation distorts the output signal, but it is very efficient. Up to 90% efficiency is possible.

A Class D amplifier is **a type of amplifier that uses switching technology to achieve high efficiency**. (E7B02) The output of a class D amplifier circuit includes **a low-pass filter to remove switching signal components**. (E7B03)

Amplifiers are used in many different applications, and in most signal quality is very important. Poorly-designed RF power amplifiers, for example, may emit harmonics or spurious signals, that may cause harmful interference.

One thing that can be done to prevent unwanted oscillations in an RF power amplifier is to **install parasitic suppressors and/or neutralize the stage**. (E7B05) An RF power amplifier can be neutralized **by feeding a 180-degree out-of-phase portion of the output back to the input**. (E7B08) Another thing one can do to reduce unwanted emissions is to use a push-pull amplifier.

In order to preserve signal integrity, amplifiers used as the final amplifier in an amateur radio transceiver, or as an external amplifier, are Class A or Class AB linear amplifiers. The use of non-linear Class C amplifiers is not a good choice. The reason for this is that **signal distortion and excessive bandwidth** is a likely result when a Class C amplifier is used to amplify a single-sideband phone signal. (E7B07)

Although transistorized linear amplifiers are becoming more common, many high-power amplifiers still use vacuum tubes. These amplifiers require that the operator tune the output circuit. **The tuning capacitor is adjusted for minimum plate current, and the loading capacitor is adjusted for maximum permissible plate current** describes how the loading and tuning capacitors are to be adjusted when tuning a vacuum tube RF power amplifier that employs a Pi-network output circuit. (E7B09)

Figure E7-1

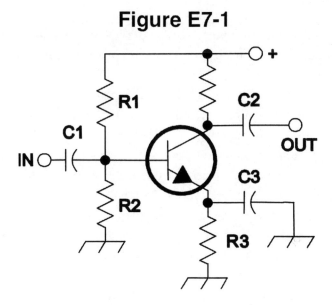

The type of circuit shown in Figure E7-1 is a **common emitter amplifier**. (E7B12) In Figure E7-1, the purpose of R1 and R2 is to provide **fixed bias**. (E7B10) In Figure E7-1, the purpose of R3 is to provide **self bias**. (E7B11)

Figure E7-2

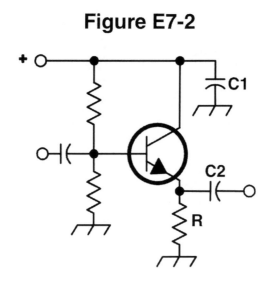

In Figure E7-2, the purpose of R is to provide **emitter load**. (E7B13) In Figure E7-2, the purpose of C2 is to provide **output coupling**. (E7B14)

Thermal runaway is one problem that can occur if a transistor amplifier is not designed correctly. What happens is that when the ambient temperature increases, the leakage current of the transistor increases, causing an increase in the collector-to-emitter current. This increases the power dissipation, further increasing the junction temperature, which increases yet again the leakage current. One way to prevent thermal runaway in a bipolar transistor amplifier is to **use a resistor in series with the emitter**. (E7B15)

RF power amplifiers often generate unwanted signals via a process called intermodulation. Strong signals external to the transmitter combine with the signal being generated, causing sometimes unexpected and unwanted emissions. The effect of intermodulation products in a linear power amplifier is the **transmission of spurious signals**. (E7B16) Odd-order, rather than even-order, intermodulation distortion products are of concern in linear power amplifiers **because they are relatively close in frequency to the desired signal**. (E7B17)

One type of amplifier that is often used as a power amplifier is the grounded-grid amplifier. Grounded-grid amplifiers are relatively easy to build, and they are very stable in operation. One characteristic of a grounded-grid amplifier is **low input impedance**. (E7B18) This is a useful characteristic because the output impedance of most amateur radio transmitters, which are used to drive these amplifiers, is 50 ohms.

E7C - Filters and matching networks: types of networks; types of filters; filter applications; filter characteristics; impedance matching; DSP filtering

Because the impedance of inductors and capacitors vary with frequency, we often make filters out of them. One of the most common is the T-network filter, so called because it looks like the letter T. An example is shown in figure E7C-1.

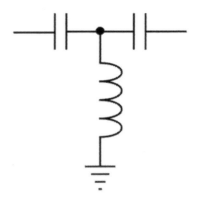

Figure E7C-1. T-network filter

This particular filter is a high-pass filter. That is to say it will pass frequencies above a certain frequency, called the cutoff frequency, and block frequencies below that frequency. A T-network with series capacitors and a parallel shunt inductor has the property of it being **a high-pass filter**. (E7C02) The reason the circuit acts this way is that as the frequency of a signal increases, capacitive reactance decreases and inductive reactance increases, meaning that lower-frequency signals are more likely to be shunted to ground.

A circuit containing capacitors and inductors can also form a low-pass filter. A low-pass filter is a circuit that passes frequencies below the cutoff frequency and blocks frequencies above it.

Pi is the common name for a filter network which is equivalent to two L networks connected back-to-back with the inductors in series and the capacitors in shunt at the input and output. (E7C11). The circuit shown in figure E7C-2 is called a pi filter because it looks like the Greek letter π.

The capacitors and inductors of a low-pass filter Pi-network are arranged such that **a capacitor is connected between the input and ground, another capacitor is connected between the output and ground, and an inductor is connected between input and output**. (E7C01) The reason the circuit acts this way is that as the frequency of a signal increases, capacitive reactance decreases and inductive reactance increases, meaning that higher-frequency signals are more likely to be shunted to ground.

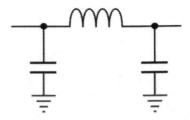

Figure E7C-2. Pi-network filter

Pi networks can also be used to match the output impedance of one circuit to the input impedance of another or the output impedance of a transmitter to the input impedance of an antenna. An impedance-matching circuit transforms a complex impedance to a resistive impedance because **it cancels the reactive part of the impedance and changes the resistive part to a desired value**. (E7C04) One advantage of a Pi matching network over an L matching network consisting of a single inductor and a single capacitor is that **the Q of Pi networks can be varied depending on the component values chosen**. (E7C13)

A Pi network with an additional series inductor on the output describes a Pi-L network used for matching a vacuum-tube final amplifier to a 50-ohm unbalanced output. (E7C12) One advantage a Pi-L-network has over a Pi-network for impedance matching between the final amplifier of a vacuum-tube transmitter and an antenna is that it has **greater harmonic suppression**. (E7C03)

Piezoelectric crystals are also used to build filters. A crystal lattice filter is **a filter with narrow bandwidth and steep skirts made using quartz crystals**. (E7C15) **The relative frequencies of the individual crystals** is the factor that has the greatest effect in helping determine the bandwidth and response shape of a crystal ladder filter. (E7C08) A "Jones filter" is **a variable bandwidth crystal lattice filter** used as part of a HF receiver IF stage. (E7C09)

Different types of filters have different characteristics. For example, a **Chebyshev filter** is a filter type described as having ripple in the passband and a sharp cutoff. (E7C05) On the other hand, the distinguishing features of an elliptical filter are **extremely sharp cutoff with one or more notches in the stop band**. (E7C06)

Filters have both amplitude and phase-response characteristics. In some applications, both are important. **Digital modes**, for example, are most affected by non-linear phase response in a receiver IF filter. (E7C14)

Often, you'll choose a filter type for a particular application. For example, to attenuate an interfering carrier signal while receiving an SSB transmission, you would use **a notch filter**. (E7C07) **A cavity filter** would be the best choice for use in a 2 meter repeater duplexer. (E7C10)

E7D - Power supplies and voltage regulators; solar array control chargers

Linear power supplies are a type of power supply used in amateur radio stations. They are called linear power supplies because they use linear voltage regulator ICs to maintain a constant output voltage. One characteristic of a linear electronic voltage regulator is **the conduction of a control element is varied to maintain a constant output voltage**. (E7D01) The control element in the circuit in Figure E7-3 below is Q1.

The device typically used as a stable reference voltage in a linear voltage regulator is **a Zener diode**. (E7D03) D1 in Figure E7-3 below is a zener diode.

A series regulator is the type of linear voltage regulator that usually makes the most efficient use of the primary power source. (E7D04) **A shunt regulator** is the type of linear voltage regulator that places a constant load on the unregulated voltage source. (E7D05)

Figure E7- 3

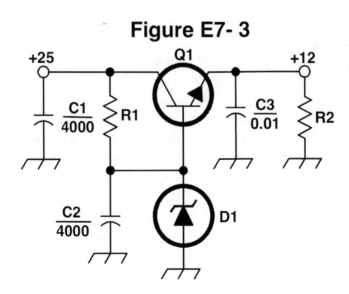

The circuit shown in Figure E7-3 is a **linear voltage regulator**. (E7D08) This is a series voltage regulator. Q1 in the circuit shown in

Figure E7-3 **increases the current-handling capability of the regulator**. (E7D06) Q1 is sometimes called a pass transistor. A **pass transistor** is the circuit element controlled by a series analog voltage regulator to maintain a constant output voltage. (E7D11) C2 in the circuit shown in Figure E7-3 **bypasses hum around D1**. (E7D07)

An important analog voltage regulator specification is the drop-out voltage. The drop-out voltage of an analog voltage regulator is the **minimum input-to-output voltage required to maintain regulation**. (E7D12) For example, if an analog voltage regulator has a drop-out voltage of 2 V, the input voltage must be at least 11 V in order to maintain an output voltage of 9 V.

Power dissipation is also important when designing a power supply with a series-connected linear voltage regulator. Excessive power dissipation reduces the efficiency of the supply and could require that you use large heat sinks to dissipate the power. The equation for calculating power dissipation by a series connected linear voltage regulator is the **voltage difference from input to output multiplied by output current**. (E7D13)

Switching power supplies

Nowadays, you are as likely to find a switching power supply in an amateur radio station as you are a linear power supply. Switching power supplies use a much different method of regulating the output voltage than a linear supply. One characteristic of a switching electronic voltage regulator is **the controlled device's duty cycle is changed to produce a constant average output voltage**. (E7D02)

Switching power supplies are usually less expensive and lighter than a linear power supply with the same output rating. Switching supplies are also generally more efficient than linear power supplies. The primary reason that a high-frequency switching type high voltage power supply can be both less expensive and lighter in weight than a conventional power supply is that **the high frequency inverter design uses much smaller transformers and filter components for an equivalent power output**. (E7D10) One disadvantage is that the circuitry in a switching supply is more complicated than the circuitry in a linear supply.

High-voltage power supplies

Most HF transceivers and VHF/UHF transceivers operate at a relatively low voltage. This is normally around 12 - 15 VDC. Some devices, such as older tube equipment and linear amplifiers need higher voltages to operate. These power supplies are quite different than the low-voltage linear and switching supplies describe above.

One difference is that the unregulated supplies used in tube equipment often have what's called a bleeder resistor. One purpose of a "bleeder" resistor in a conventional (unregulated) power supply is **to improve output voltage regulation**. (E7D14)

High-voltage supplies may also have a step-start circuit. The purpose of a "step-start" circuit in a high-voltage power supply is **to allow the filter capacitors to charge gradually**. (E7D15)

When several electrolytic filter capacitors are connected in series to increase the operating voltage of a power supply filter circuit, resistors should be connected across each capacitor:

- To equalize, as much as possible, the voltage drop across each capacitor
- To provide a safety bleeder to discharge the capacitors when the supply is off
- To provide a minimum load current to reduce voltage excursions at light loads

All of these choices are correct. (E7D16)

Solar array charge controllers

Solar array charge controllers are voltage or current regulators that are used when charging batteries from a solar array. The main reason to use a charge controller with a solar power system is the **prevention of battery damage due to overcharge**. (E7D09) Most solar panels that are rated at 12 V actually output 16 to 20 V, and if that output is not regulated, batteries connected to the solar panel may be damaged from overcharging.

E7E - Modulation and demodulation: reactance, phase and balanced modulators; detectors; mixer stages

Modulation is the process of adding information, such as voice or digital information, to a carrier signal. The most common types of modulation that we use in amateur radio are amplitude modulation (AM) and frequency modulation (FM). Single-sideband, or SSB, is a form of amplitude modulation.

To frequency modulate a carrier, a transmitter will sometimes use a modulator that varies the phase of the signal. This is sometimes called phase modulation (PM). One way to generate FM phone emissions is to use **a reactance modulator on the oscillator.** (E7E01) The function of a reactance modulator is **to produce PM signals by using an electrically variable inductance or capacitance.** (E7E02) An analog phase modulator functions **by varying the tuning of an amplifier tank circuit to produce PM signals.** (E7E03)

To boost the higher audio frequencies, **a pre-emphasis network** is often added to an FM transmitter. (E7E05) **For compatibility with transmitters using phase modulation,** de-emphasis is commonly used in FM communications receivers. (E7E06)

Amplitude modulation and single-sideband signals are produced using mixer circuits. The carrier frequency and the baseband signals are input to the mixer circuit which produces an amplitude modulated output. The term baseband in radio communications refers to **the frequency components present in the modulating signal.** (E7E07) The principal frequencies that appear at the output of a mixer circuit are **the two input frequencies along with their sum and difference frequencies.** (E7E08)

When using a mixer, you must take care not to use too high of a signal at the inputs. **Spurious mixer products are generated** when an excessive amount of signal energy reaches a mixer circuit. (E7E09)

Single sideband is most often used for phone transmission on the HF bands and for weak-signal operation on the VHF and UHF bands. One way a single-sideband phone signal can be generated is **by using a balanced modulator followed by a filter.** (E7E04) A balanced modulator is a type of mixer. The output of a balanced modulator, however, does not contain the carrier frequency, only the two sidebands.

At the receiving station, a modulated signal has to be demodulated. Amplitude modulated signals are often demodulated using a diode detector circuit. A diode detector functions **by rectification and filtering of RF signals**. (E7E10)

For demodulating SSB signals, you want something a little more sophisticated. A **product detector** is a type of detector that is well suited for demodulating SSB signals. (E7E11) A product detector is actually a frequency mixer. It takes the product of the modulated signal and a local oscillator, hence the name. In an FM receiver, **the circuit for detecting FM signals** is a frequency discriminator. (E7E12)

E7F - DSP filtering and other operations; Software Defined Radio fundamentals; DSP modulation and demodulation

Some modern radios modulate and demodulate signals entirely in software. This type of radio is called a software-defined radio, or SDR. One type of SDR uses a process called direct digital conversion to convert the analog radio signal into a series of numbers. As applied to software defined radios, direct digital conversion means **incoming RF is digitized by an analog-to-digital converter without being mixed with a local oscillator signal**. (E7F01)

Analog-to-digital converter specifications are crucial for a software-defined radio. For example, **sample rate** is the aspect of receiver analog-to-digital conversion that determines the maximum receive bandwidth of a Direct Digital Conversion SDR. (E7F10) An analog signal must be sampled **at twice the rate of the highest frequency component of the signal** by an analog-to-digital converter so that the signal can be accurately reproduced. (E7F05)

Voltage resolution is also important. The **reference voltage level and sample width in bits** sets the minimum detectable signal level for an SDR in the absence of atmospheric or thermal noise. (E7F11) The minimum number of bits required for an analog-to-digital converter to sample a signal with a range of 1 volt at a resolution of 1 millivolt is **10 bits**. (E7F06)

Modern software defined radios convert an incoming signal into two data streams: I and Q. The letters I and Q in I/Q modulation (and demodulation) represent **In-phase and Quadrature**. (E7F17). The I and Q data streams are 90 degrees out of phase with one another, and as a result, the two data streams not only show how the amplitude of a signal is changing, but how the phase of a signal is changing.

The digital process that is applied to I and Q signals in order to recover the baseband modulation information is the **Fast Fourier Transform**. (E7F12) **Converting digital signals from the time domain to the frequency domain** is the function that a Fast Fourier Transform performs. (E7F07)

Once a signal has been digitized, or converted into a series of numbers, it can be digitally filtered. The kind of digital signal processing audio filter that removes unwanted noise from a received SSB signal is **an adaptive filter**. (E7F02) Another type of digital filter that is often used in a direct digital conversion receiver is the finite impulse, or FIR, filter. An advantage of a Finite Impulse Response (FIR) filter vs an Infinite Impulse Response (IIR) digital filter is that **FIR filters delay all frequency components of the signal by the same amount**. (E7F15)

The FIR filter in a software defined radio might also be a decimating filter. The decimation function **reduces the effective sample rate by removing samples** when using a digital filter. (E7F08) SDRs perform decimation because the signal of interest will usually have a significantly lower bandwidth than the digitized signal, and reducing the sample rate allows SDRs to use less-powerful processors. One way the sampling rate of an existing digital signal might be adjusted by a factor of 3/4 is to **interpolate by a factor of three, then decimate by a factor of four**. (E7F16)

An anti-aliasing digital filter is required in a digital decimator because **it removes high-frequency signal components which would otherwise be reproduced as lower frequency components**. (E7F09)

Taps in a digital signal processing filter **provide incremental signal delays for filter algorithms**. (E7F13) **More taps** would allow a digital signal processing filter to create a sharper filter response. (E7F14)

Signals can also be generated using SDR techniques. A common method of generating an SSB signal using digital signal processing is to **combine signals with a quadrature phase relationship**. (E7F04) The type of digital signal processing filter used to generate an SSB signal is **a Hilbert-transform filter**. (E7F03)

E7G - Active filters and op-amps: active audio filters; characteristics; basic circuit design; operational amplifiers

Operational amplifiers, or op-amps for short, are very versatile components. They can be used to build amplifiers, filter circuits, and many other types of circuits that do analog signal processing.

An integrated circuit operational amplifier is **a high-gain, direct-coupled differential amplifier with very high input and very low output impedance**. (E7G12) The typical input impedance of an integrated circuit op-amp is **very high**. (E7G03) The typical output impedance of an integrated circuit op-amp is **very low**. (E7G01)

The gain of an ideal operational amplifier **does not vary with frequency**. (E7G08) Most op amps aren't ideal, though. While some modern op amps can be used at high frequencies, many of the older ones can't be used at frequencies above a couple of MHz.

Ideally, with no input signal, there should be no voltage difference between the two input terminals, and the output voltage should also be zero. Since no electronic component is ideal, there will be a voltage between these two terminals. We call this the input offset voltage. Put another way, the op-amp input-offset voltage is **the differential input voltage needed to bring the open-loop output voltage to zero**. (E7G04)

Because they are active components—that is to say that they amplify—filters made with op amps are called active filters. The most appropriate use of an op-amp active filter is **as an audio filter in a receiver**. (E7G06). The values of capacitors and resistors external to the op-amp primarily determine the gain and frequency characteristics of an op-amp RC active filter.

Ringing is one undesirable characteristic of an op-amp filter. One effect of ringing in a filter is that **undesired oscillations to be added to the desired signal**. (E7G02) One way to prevent unwanted ringing and audio instability in a multi-section op-amp RC audio filter circuit is to **restrict both gain and Q**. (E7G05)

Calculating the gain of an op amp circuit is relatively straightforward. The gain is simply R_F/R_{in}. In figure E7-4 below, R_{in} =

R_1. Therefore, the magnitude of voltage gain that can be expected from the circuit in Figure E7-4 when R1 is 10 ohms and R_F is 470 ohms is 470/10, or **47**. (E7G07) The absolute voltage gain that can be expected from the circuit in Figure E7-4 when R1 is 1800 ohms and R_F is 68 kilohms is 68,000/1,800, or **38**. (E7G10) The absolute voltage gain that can be expected from the circuit in Figure E7-4 when R1 is 3300 ohms and R_F is 47 kilohms is 47,000/3,300, or **14**. (E7G11)

Figure E7-4

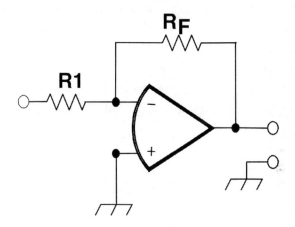

-2.3 volts will be the output voltage of the circuit shown in Figure E7-4 if R1 is 1000 ohms, R_F is 10,000 ohms, and 0.23 volts dc is applied to the input. (E7G09) The gain of the circuit will be 10,000/1,000 or 10, and the output voltage will be equal to the input voltage times the gain. 0.23 V x 10 = 2.3 V, but since the input voltage is being applied to the negative input, the output voltage will be negative.

E7H - Oscillators and signal sources: types of oscillators; synthesizers and phase-locked loops; direct digital synthesizers; stabilizing thermal drift; microphonics; high accuracy oscillators

Oscillator circuits are one of the basic building blocks of amateur radio equipment. Oscillator circuits are not only used to generate the signals we transmit, they are also an integral part of receivers, such as the superheterodyne receiver.

You can think of an oscillator as an amplifier with a tuned circuit that provides positive feedback. This tuned circuit might be an LC circuit or a crystal. The values of the components in the tuned circuit determine the output frequency of the oscillator. There are three types of oscillator circuits commonly used in Amateur Radio equipment - **Colpitts, Hartley and Pierce.** (E7H01) **Colpitts and Hartley** oscillator circuits are commonly used in VFOs. (E7H06)

In a Hartley oscillator (shown in the figure below), positive feedback is supplied **through a tapped coil.** (E7H03)

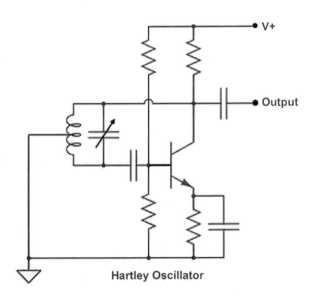

Hartley Oscillator

In a Colpitts oscillator, positive feedback is supplied **through a capacitive divider**. (E7H04)

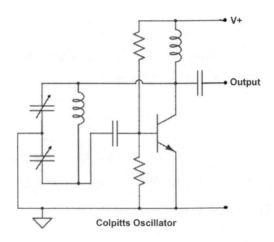

Colpitts Oscillator

In a Pierce oscillator, positive feedback is supplied **through a quartz crystal**. (E7H05) To ensure that a crystal oscillator provides the frequency specified by the crystal manufacturer, you must **provide the crystal with a specified parallel capacitance**. (E7H12)

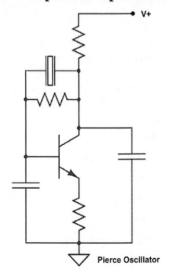

Pierce Oscillator

One problem that can occur with oscillators that use LC circuits is that their output frequency drifts because as the capacitors heat up their values change and the resonant frequency of the LC circuit changes. This phenomenon is called thermal drift. **NPO capacitors** are components that can be used to reduce thermal drift in crystal oscillators. (E7H08) The capacitance of NPO capacitors changes very little over normal operating temperatures.

Another problem that oscillators sometimes have is called microphonics. **Changes in oscillator frequency due to mechanical vibration** describes a microphonic. (E7H02) An oscillator's microphonic responses can be reduced by **mechanically isolating the oscillator from its enclosure**. (EH707)

Digital frequency synthesizers

Most modern amateur radio transceivers use digital frequency synthesizers instead of analog oscillators to generate RF signals. One reason for this is that they are much more stable than analog oscillators. The two main types of digital frequency synthesizers are the direct digital synthesizer and the phase-locked loop synthesizer.

A direct digital synthesizer is the type of frequency synthesizer circuit that uses a phase accumulator, lookup table, digital to analog converter and a low-pass anti-alias filter. (E7H09) The information contained in the lookup table of a direct digital frequency synthesizer a r e **the amplitude values that represent a sine-wave output**. (E7H10)

Frequency synthesizers that use phase-locked loops are also popular. A phase-locked loop circuit is **an electronic servo loop consisting of a phase detector, a low-pass filter, a voltage-controlled oscillator, and a stable reference oscillator**. (E7H14) **Frequency synthesis, FM demodulation** are two functions that can be performed by a phase-locked loop. (E7H15)

Both direct digital synthesizers and phase-locked loop synthesizers have issues with spectral purity. The major spectral impurity components of direct digital synthesizers are **spurious signals at discrete frequencies**. (E7H11)

Because frequency multipliers are often used for generating RF signals at microwave frequencies, it is very important that the oscillators used in microwave transmitters are accurate and stable. Any inaccuracy or instability will be multiplied along with the desired frequency. **All of these choices are correct** when talking about techniques for providing highly accurate and stable oscillators needed for microwave transmission and reception: (E7H13)

- Use a GPS signal reference
- Use a rubidium stabilized reference oscillator
- Use a temperature-controlled high Q dielectric resonator

E8: SIGNALS AND EMISSIONS

E8A - AC waveforms: sine, square, sawtooth and irregular waveforms; AC measurements; average and PEP of RF signals; Fourier analysis; Analog to digital conversion: Digital to Analog conversion

We use all different kinds of waveforms in amateur radio. It is, therefore, important to know about the different types of waveforms and how to measure their parameters. One parameter of an AC waveform that you need to know is its root mean square, or RMS, value. The root-mean-square value of an AC voltage is the DC voltage causing the same amount of heating in a resistor as the corresponding RMS AC voltage. Because of this, the most accurate way of measuring the RMS voltage of a complex waveform would be **measuring the heating effect in a known resistor**. (E8A05)

If the waveform is regular, it's relatively easy to calculate the RMS value. In the case of a sine wave, the RMS value is 0.707 times the peak value. You use the RMS voltage value to calculate the power of a wave.

The type of waveform produced by human speech is, however, irregular. For irregular waveforms, such as that of a single-sideband phone signal, we're most interested in the peak envelope power (PEP). **The characteristics of the modulating signal** determine the

PEP-to-average power ratio of a single-sideband phone signal. (E8A07) This makes calculating or measuring the average power more difficult.

If you know the peak envelope power (PEP), though, you can make a pretty good guess at the average power. The approximate ratio of PEP-to-average power in a typical single-sideband phone signal is **2.5 to 1**. (E8A06) Put another way, the average power of an SSB signal is about 40% of the peak power.

· It used to be that all the waveforms we used in amateur radio were analog waveforms, but nowadays digital waveforms may be even more important than analog waveforms. An advantage of using digital signals instead of analog signals to convey the same information is that **digital signals can be regenerated multiple times without error**. (E8A12) **All of these choices are correct** when talking about the types of information that can be conveyed using digital waveforms (E8A11):

- Human speech
- Video signals
- Data

Perhaps the most common digital wave form is the square wave. An ideal square wave alternates regularly and instantaneously between two different values. An interesting fact is that **a square wave** is the type of wave that is made up of a sine wave plus all of its odd harmonics. (E8A01)

Another type of wave used in amateur radio is the sawtooth wave. **A sawtooth wave** is the type of wave that has a rise time significantly faster than its fall time (or vice versa). (E8A02) The type of wave made up of sine waves of a given fundamental frequency plus all its harmonics is **a sawtooth wave**. (E8A03)

To make use of digital techniques in amateur radio, such as digital signal processing or DSP, we must convert analog signals to digital signals and vice-versa. To do this we use an analog-to-digital converter (ADC).

ADCs sample a signal at a particular point in time and convert that sample into a digital number that is proportional to the amplitude at that time. The number of bits in the digital number is called the resolution of the ADC. An analog-to-digital converter with 8 bit resolution can encode **256** levels. (E8A09)

To convert radio signals to digital streams used in software-defined radios, you need to sample the signal at a very high rate in order to preserve signal integrity. A direct or flash conversion analog-to-digital converter would, therefore, be useful for a software defined radio because its **very high speed allows digitizing high frequencies**. (E8A08)

Sequential sampling is one of the methods commonly used to convert analog signals to digital signals. (E8A13) Sequential sampling allows you to sample a signal only once per cycle, thereby allowing you to use a slower, and less expensive ADC, and still preserve signal integrity. Sequential sampling only works, however, when the waveform is a regular waveform.

Sometimes signals are passed through a low pass filter before being digitized. The purpose of a low pass filter used in conjunction with a digital-to-analog converter is to **remove harmonics from the output caused by the discrete analog levels generated**. (E8A10)

The differential nonlinearity in the ADC's encoder transfer function can be reduced by the proper use of dither. With respect to analog to digital converters, dither is **a small amount of noise added to the input signal to allow more precise representation of a signal over time**. (E8A04)

E8B - Modulation and demodulation: modulation methods; modulation index and deviation ratio; frequency and time division multiplexing; Orthogonal Frequency Division Multiplexing

In FM modulation, the two primary parameters of interest are deviation ratio and modulation index. Deviation ratio is **the ratio of the maximum carrier frequency deviation to the highest audio modulating frequency**. (E8B09) The deviation ratio of an FM-phone signal having a maximum frequency swing of plus-or-minus 5 kHz when the maximum modulation frequency is 3 kHz is **1.67**. (E8B05) The deviation ratio of an FM phone signal having a maximum frequency swing of plus or minus 7.5 kHz when the maximum modulation frequency is 3.5 kHz is **2.14**. (E8B06)

The term for the ratio between the frequency deviation of an RF carrier wave, and the modulating frequency of its corresponding FM-phone signal is **modulation index**. (E8B01) The modulation index is equal to the ratio of the frequency deviation to the modulating frequency. The modulation index of a phase-modulated emission **does not depend on the RF carrier frequency**. (E8B02)

The modulation index of an FM-phone signal having a maximum frequency deviation of 3000 Hz either side of the carrier frequency, when the modulating frequency is 1000 Hz is **3**. (E8B03) The modulation index of an FM-phone signal having a maximum carrier deviation of plus or minus 6 kHz when modulated with a 2-kHz modulating frequency is **3**. (E8B04)

Some communications systems use multiplexing techniques to combine several separate analog information streams into a single analog radio frequency signal. When a system uses frequency division multiplexing, **two or more information streams are merged into a "baseband," which then modulates the transmitter**. (E8B10). When a system uses digital time division multiplexing, **two or more signals are arranged to share discrete time slots of a data transmission**. (E8B11)

Orthogonal Frequency Division Multiplexing is a technique used f o r **high speed digital modes**. (E8B07) Orthogonal Frequency

Division Multiplexing is **a digital modulation technique using subcarriers at frequencies chosen to avoid intersymbol interference.** (E8B08)

E8C - Digital signals: digital communications modes; information rate vs. bandwidth; error correction

Digital modes have become very popular in amateur radio lately, but Morse Code, the type of modulation that has been around the longest, is the original digital mode. One advantage of using Morse Code is that it has a very narrow bandwidth. The bandwidth necessary for a 13-WPM international Morse code transmission is **approximately 52 Hz.** (E8C05)

The bandwidth needed for digital transmissions increases as the data rate increases. The formula for calculating the bandwidth, given the baud rate and frequency shift is:

BW (Hz) = frequency shift x 1.2 + baud rate

Using this equation, we see that the bandwidth necessary for a 170-hertz shift, 300-baud ASCII transmission is **0.5 kHz.** (E8C06) The bandwidth necessary for a 4800-Hz frequency shift, 9600-baud ASCII FM transmission is **15.36 kHz.** (E8C07)

PSK has become a very popular digital mode. One reason for this is that it occupies a very narrow bandwidth - only 31 Hz. One technique used to minimize the bandwidth requirements of a PSK31 signal is the **use of sinusoidal data pulses.** (E8C04) When performing phase shift keying, it is also advantageous to shift phase precisely at the zero crossing of the RF carrier because **this results in the least possible transmitted bandwidth for the particular mode.** (E8C03)

When digital communication systems were first developed, data was sent one bit at a time. As the need for faster data transmission grew, engineers figured out how to send multiple bit simultaneously. Instead of sending single bits, these systems send and receive "symbols," which represent multiple bits. The definition of symbol rate in a digital transmission is **the rate at which the waveform of a transmitted signal changes to convey information.** (E8C02) The relationship between symbol rate and baud is **they are the same.** (E8C11)

Whenever digital data is sent over a radio channel, it is encoded. Gray codes are often used for this purpose. **Gray code** is the name of a digital code where each preceding or following character changes by only one bit. (E8C09) An advantage of Gray code in digital communications where symbols are transmitted as multiple bits is that **it facilitates error detection**. (E8C10)

There are many things that can cause errors in a data stream. For example, an interfering signal might cause a receiver to interpret a transmitted symbol incorrectly. When these errors are not allowable, digital communications systems implement some form of error detection and correction.

One way to achieve reliable data communication is to use the Automatic Repeat ReQuest, or ARQ, protocol. In systems that use ARQ error control, **if errors are detected, a retransmission is requested**. (E8C08) Senders will also re-transmit a data packet if they do not receive an acknowledgement from the receiver that it has correctly received a packet.

Another way to correct errors is a technique called forward error correction. Forward Error Correction is implemented **by transmitting extra data that may be used to detect and correct transmission errors**. (E8C01) When a receiver receives erroneous data, it can correct the errors itself.

E8D - Keying defects and overmodulation of digital signals; digital codes; spread spectrum

It is good amateur practice to ensure that the CW and digital signals you transmit are high quality. Perhaps the biggest problem that you'll have when sending CW signals is key clicks. Key clicks are spurious signals that cause interference to other stations operating near your frequency. **The generation of key clicks** is the primary effect of extremely short rise or fall time on a CW signal. (E8D04) It follows, then that the most common method of reducing key clicks is to **reduce keying waveform rise and fall times**. (E8D05) Fortunately, most modern transceivers allow you to set the rise and fall times of the CW signal, so this is an easy fix.

To ensure high-quality digital signals, such as when transmitting audio frequency shift signals, such as PSK31, you need to set the audio input level properly. A common cause of overmodulation of AFSK signals is **excessive transmit audio levels**. (E8D07). **Strong ALC action** indicates likely overmodulation of an AFSK signal such as PSK or MFSK. (E8D06)

Intermodulation Distortion (IMD) is a parameter that you can measure that might indicate that excessively high input levels are causing distortion in an AFSK signal. (E8D08) A good minimum IMD level for an idling PSK signal is **-30 dB**. (E8D09)

Digital codes

Although ASCII and Unicode have now become standard codes for sending textual information, we still use the Baudot code when sending and receiving RTTY. Some of the differences between the Baudot digital code and ASCII are that **Baudot uses 5 data bits per character, ASCII uses 7 or 8; Baudot uses 2 characters as letters/figures shift codes, ASCII has no letters/figures shift code**. (E8D10)

Even though it uses more bits per character, ASCII does have some advantages over Baudot. For example, one advantage of using ASCII code for data communications is that **it is possible to transmit both upper and lower case text**. (E8D11)

In an eight-bit ASCII character, the eighth bit is the parity bit. In systems that use even parity, the parity bit is set to either a one or a zero, so that the number of ones in the character is equal to an even number. In systems that use odd parity, the parity bit is set to either a one or a zero, so that the number of ones in the character is equal to an odd number. The advantage of including a parity bit with an ASCII character stream is that **some types of errors can be detected**. (E8D12)

Spread spectrum

Amateurs can now use spread-spectrum techniques on all bands above 420 MHz. The reason these bands are used is because spread-spectrum signals require more bandwidth than is available on the lower frequency bands.

Spread spectrum transmissions generally change frequency during a transmission. This is called frequency hopping. The way the spread spectrum technique of frequency hopping works is that **the frequency of the transmitted signal is changed very rapidly according to a particular sequence also used by the receiving station.** (E8D03) **Direct sequence** is a spread spectrum communications technique that uses a high speed binary bit stream to shift the phase of an RF carrier. (E8D02)

Because transmission and reception occur over a wide band of frequencies, spread spectrum communications are less susceptible to interference on a single frequency than are more conventional systems. Received spread spectrum signals are resistant to interference because **signals not using the spread spectrum algorithm are suppressed in the receiver.** (E8D01)

E9: ANTENNAS AND TRANSMISSION LINES

E9A Basic antenna parameters: radiation resistance, gain, beamwidth, efficiency, beamwidth; effective radiated power, polarization

Antenna gain is one of the most misunderstood topics in amateur radio. There are several reasons for this, including:

- Antennas don't really have gain in the same way that an amplifier has gain. When you use a linear amplifier, you get more power out than you put in. Since transmitting antennas are passive devices, there's no way to get more power out than you put in.

- It's not easy to measure antenna gain. There is no antenna gain meter that you can simply hook up to an antenna to measure its gain.

So, what is meant by antenna gain? Antenna gain is **the ratio of the radiated signal strength of an antenna in the direction of maximum radiation to that of a reference antenna.** (E9A07) What this means is that when you talk about antenna gain, you have to know what kind of antenna you're comparing it to.

When talking about antenna gain, antenna engineers often refer to the "isotropic antenna." An isotropic antenna is **a theoretical antenna used as a reference for antenna gain**. (E9A01) An **isotropic antenna** is an antenna that has no gain in any direction. (E9A02) That is to say it radiates the power input to it equally well in all directions.

Let's take a look at a practical example. The 1/2-wavelength dipole antenna is the most basic amateur radio antenna. The dipole actually has some gain over isotropic antenna. The reason for this is that it is directional. The signal strength transmitted broadside to the antenna will be greater than the signal strength transmitted off the ends of the antenna.

The gain of a 1/2-wavelength dipole in free space compared to an isotropic antenna is 2.15 dB. Sometimes, you'll see this value as 2.15 dBi, where dBi denotes that an isotropic antenna is being used for this comparison.

Since the isotropic antenna is a theoretical antenna, some think it's better to compare an antenna to a dipole antenna. An antenna will have a gain **3.85 dB** compared to a 1/2-wavelength dipole when it has 6 dB gain over an isotropic antenna. (E9A12) You obtain this value by simply subtracting 2.15 dB from the 6 dB figure:

Gain over a dipole = gain over an isotropic antenna - 2.15 dB = 6 dBi - 2.15 dBi = 3.85 dBd

Sometimes, the gain over a dipole is denoted as dBd.

Similarly, an antenna has a gain of **9.85 dB** compared to a 1/2-wavelength dipole when it has 12 dB gain over an isotropic antenna. (E9A13):

Gain over a dipole = gain over an isotropic antenna - 2.15 dB = 12 dBi - 2.15 dBi = 9.85 dBd

Antennas that are said to have gain are really focusing the energy that is input to them. The higher the gain, the narrower the focus, or beamwidth. The beamwidth of an antenna **decreases** as the gain is increased. (E9A06)

Effective radiated power

When you use an antenna that has gain, you are increasing the effectiveness of the power input to it, at least in the direction the antenna is pointing. The term that describes station output, taking into account all gains and losses is **effective radiated power**. (E9A18) The effective radiated power is not just the input power times the gain of the antenna. You also have to take into account losses in other parts of the antenna system.

This is especially true for VHF and UHF repeater systems, where losses in the feedline, duplexer, and circulator can be significant. The power that reaches the antenna may be substantially lower than the power output of the transmitter.

For example, the effective radiated power relative to a dipole of a repeater station with 150 watts transmitter power output, 2 dB feed line loss, 2.2 dB duplexer loss, and 7 dBd antenna gain is **286 watts**. (E9A15) To calculate the answer, you have to first subtract the losses from the gain, as expressed in dB to get the total gain of the system:

total system gain = 7 dB – 2 dB – 2.2 dB = 2.8 dB.

Now, recall that 3 dB corresponds to a power ration of 2:1, as shown in the table below. 2.8 dB would then be slight less than that. In fact, 2.8dB corresponds to a power ratio of approximately 1.905, so the effective radiated power is the transmitter output power times the total system gain:

effective radiated power = 150 W x 1.905 = 268 W.

dB	Gain	Loss
3	X2	X1/2
6	X4	X1/4
10	X10	X1/10

Let's look at another example. The effective radiated power relative to a dipole of a repeater station with 200 watts transmitter power output, 4 dB feed line loss, 3.2 dB duplexer loss, 0.8 dB circulator loss, and 10 dBd antenna gain is **317 watts**. (E9A16). In this case, the total gain of the system is 10 dB − 4 dB − 3.2 dB − 0.8 dB, or 2.0 dB. 2.0 dB corresponds to a power ratio of approximately 1.585, and the effective radiated power equals 200 W x 1.585 = 317 W. In this system, high feedline and duplexer losses are almost completely negating the benefit of using such a high gain antenna.

Finally, the effective radiated power of a repeater station with 200 watts transmitter power output, 2 dB feed line loss, 2.8 dB duplexer loss, 1.2 dB circulator loss, and 7 dBi antenna gain is **252 watts**. (E9A17) In this example, the total gain of the system is 7 dB − 2 dB − 2.8 dB − 1.2 dB, or 1.0 dB. 1.0 dB corresponds to a power ratio of approximately 1.26, and the effective radiated power equals 200 W x 1.26 = 252 W.

Feedpoint impedance, antenna efficiency, frequency range, beamwidth

Other antenna parameters are also important, of courese. One of the most basic antenna parameters is the feedpoint impedance. Why would one need to know the feed point impedance of an antenna? **To match impedances in order to minimize standing wave ratio on the transmission line**. (E9A03) The reason that it's important to minimize the standing wave ratio, or SWR, is that if you're using coaxial cables, minimizing the SWR will also help you minimize losses. If you minimize losses, you'll radiate more signal.

Many factors may affect the feed point impedance of an antenna, including **antenna height, conductor length/diameter ratio and location of nearby conductive objects**. (E9A04) For example, we say that the feedpoint impedance of a half-wavelength, dipole antenna is 72 Ω, but that's only really true if the antenna is in free space. When it's closer to the ground than a quarter wavelength, then the impedance will be different. That's why you have to tune the antenna when you install it.

Radiation resistance

Another antenna parameter that's frequently discussed is radiation resistance. The radiation resistance of an antenna is **the value of a resistance that would dissipate the same amount of power as that radiated from an antenna.** (E9A14) **Radiation resistance plus ohmic resistance** is included in the total resistance of an antenna system. (E9A05)

If you know the radiation resistance and the ohmic resistance of an antenna, you can calculate its efficiency. You calculate antenna efficiency with the formula **(radiation resistance / total resistance) x 100 percent.** (E9A09)

Vertical antennas are sometimes criticized as being inefficient antennas. **Soil conductivity** is one factor that determines ground losses for a ground-mounted vertical antenna operating in the 3-30 MHz range. (E9A11) If soil conductivity is poor, ohmic resistance will be high, and the antenna's efficiency will be low. One way to improve the efficiency of a ground-mounted quarter-wave vertical antenna is to **install a good radial system.** (E9A10)

The frequency range over which an antenna satisfies a performance requirement is called antenna bandwidth. (E9A08) Normally, the performance requirement is an SWR of 2:1 or less. In fact, you'll sometimes hear this parameter referred to as the 2:1 SWR bandwidth.

E9B - Antenna patterns: E and H plane patterns; gain as a function of pattern; antenna design

Many amateurs use directional antennas because they are said to have "gain." When this term is used, what it means is that a directional antenna will output more power in a particular direction than an antenna that is not directional. This only makes sense; You can't get more power out of an antenna than you put in. Assuming each is driven by the same amount of power, the total amount of radiation emitted by a directional gain antenna compared with the total amount of radiation emitted from an isotropic antenna **is the same.** (E9B07)

To evaluate the performance of directional antennas, manufacturers will measure the field strength at various points in a circle around the antenna and plot those field strengths, creating a chart called the azimuth antenna radiation pattern. Figure E9-1 is a typical azimuth antenna radiation pattern.

Figure E9-1

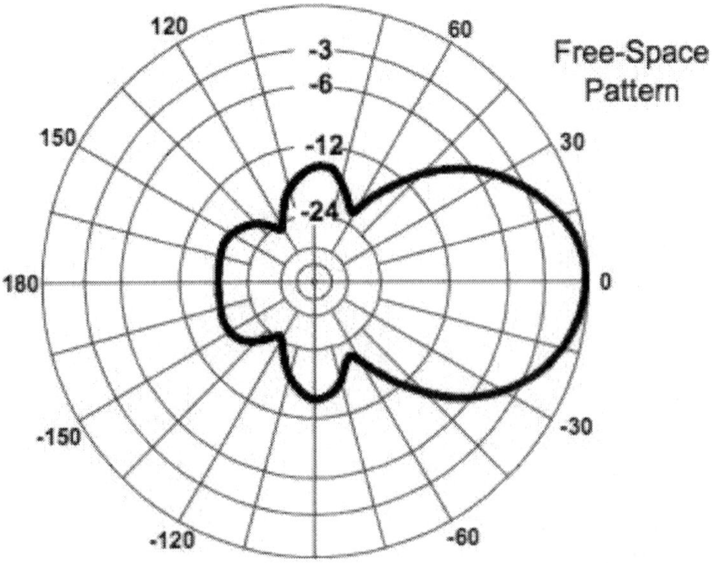

The antenna radiation pattern shows the relative strength of the signal generated by an antenna in its "far field." The far-field of an antenna is **the region where the shape of the antenna pattern is independent of distance**. (E9B12)

From the antenna radiation pattern, we can tell a bunch of things about the antenna. One of them is beamwidth. Beamwidth is a measure of the width of the main lobe of the radiation pattern. To determine the approximate beamwidth in a given plane of a directional antenna, **note the two points where the signal strength of the antenna is 3 dB less than maximum and compute the angular difference**. (E9B08) In the antenna radiation pattern shown in Figure E9-1, **50 degrees** is the 3-dB beamwidth. (E9B01)

Another parameter that's important for a directional antenna is the front-to-back ratio. The front-to-back ratio is a measure of how directional an antenna is. The higher this ratio, the more directional the antenna. In the antenna radiation pattern shown in Figure E9-1, **18 dB** is the front-to-back ratio. (E9B02)

A similar parameter is the front-to-side ratio. In the antenna radiation pattern shown in Figure E9-1, the front-to-side ratio is **14 dB**. (E9B03)

When reviewing an antenna radiation pattern, you need to remember that the field strength measurements were taken at a particular frequency. When a directional antenna is operated at different frequencies within the band for which it was designed, **the gain may change depending on frequency**. (E9B04)

Many different design factors affect these antenna parameters. For example, if the boom of a Yagi antenna is lengthened and the elements are properly retuned, what usually occurs is that **the gain increases**. (E9B06)

Because antennas radiate in three dimensions, the azimuth antenna pattern tells only part of the story. To get a complete picture of antenna performance, you also want to know what the antenna pattern is in the vertical direction. This type of pattern is called the elevation antenna pattern. An **elevation** antenna patter over real ground is show in Figure E9-2. (E9B05)

Figure E9-2

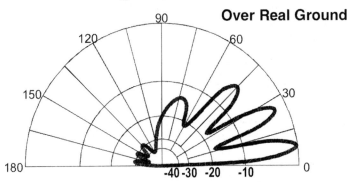

Over Real Ground

In the antenna radiation pattern shown in Figure E9-2, **4** elevation lobes appear in the forward direction. (E9B16) In the antenna radiation pattern shown in Figure E9-2, the elevation angle of peak response in is **7.5 degrees**. (E9B06) The front-to-back ratio of the radiation pattern shown in Figure E9-2 is **28 dB**. (E9B15)

Antenna design

To help design antennas, many amateurs use antenna modeling programs. **All of these choices are correct** when talking about the information obtained by submitting the details of a proposed new antenna to a modeling program (E9B14):

- SWR vs. frequency charts
- Polar plots of the far-field elevation and azimuth patterns
- Antenna gain

The type of computer program technique commonly used for modeling antennas is **method of moments**. (E9B09) The principle behind a method of moments analysis is that **a wire is modeled as a series of segments, each having a uniform value of current**. (E9B10)

The more segments your simulation uses, the more accurate the results. The problem with using too many segments, though, is that the program will take a very long time to run. You don't want to use too few segments, though. A disadvantage of decreasing the number of wire segments in an antenna model below the guideline of 10 segments per half-wavelength is that **the computed feed point impedance may be incorrect**. (E9B11)

The abbreviation NEC stands for **Numerical Electromagnetics Code** when applied to antenna modeling programs. (E9B13) This is different from the more common definition of NEC, which is the National Electrical Code.

E9C - Wire and phased array antennas: rhombic antennas; effects of ground reflections; take-off angles; Practical wire antennas: Zepps, OCFD, loops

There are many ways to put up antennas that are directional. Yagis are directional antennas, but they require a structure, such as a tower, to get them high in the air. One way to get directionality without a tower is to use phased vertical arrays.

In general, the phased vertical array consists of two or more quarter-wave vertical antennas. The radiation pattern that the array will have depends on how you feed the vertical antennas.

So, for example, the radiation pattern of two 1/4-wavelength vertical antennas spaced 1/2-wavelength apart and fed 180 degrees out of phase is **a figure-8 oriented along the axis of the array**. (E9C01) The radiation pattern of two 1/4-wavelength vertical antennas spaced 1/4-wavelength apart and fed 90 degrees out of phase is **a cardioid**. (E9C02) The radiation pattern of two 1/4-wavelength vertical antennas spaced 1/2-wavelength apart and fed in phase is **a Figure-8 broadside to the axis of the array**. (E9C03)

How and where you install an antenna affects its radiation pattern. For example, the far-field elevation pattern of a vertically polarized antenna is affected when it is mounted over seawater versus rocky ground. What happens is that **the low-angle radiation increases**. (E9C11) The main effect of placing a vertical antenna over an imperfect ground is that **it reduces low-angle radiation**. (E9C13)

Placement also affects horizontally-polarized antennas. If you compare the performance of a horizontally polarized antenna mounted on the side of a hill with the same antenna mounted on flat ground, you will find that **the main lobe takeoff angle decreases in the downhill direction**. (E9C14) The radiation pattern of a horizontally polarized 3-element beam antenna will also vary as you change its height above ground. What happens is that **the main lobe takeoff angle decreases with increasing height**. (E9C15)

Wire antennas

There are many different kinds of wire antennas. Some of the more popular are the long-wire antenna, the folded dipole antenna, the off-center fed dipole antenna, the Zepp antenna, and the G5RV antenna.

The long-wire antenna, as the name implies, is just a long piece of wire, as long as you can make it, strung up as high as you can string it. An antenna tuner is almost always required to match the impedance at the end of the long wire to the 50 Ω output of the transmitter. The radiation pattern of a long-wire antenna is very unpredictable. What happens to the radiation pattern of an unterminated long wire antenna as the wire length is increased is that **the lobes align more in the direction of the wire**. (E9C04)

The folded dipole is a variation on the basic half-wave dipole antenna. A folded dipole antenna is **a dipole consisting of one wavelength of wire forming a very thin loop**. (E9C08) The approximate feed point impedance at the center of a two-wire folded dipole antenna is **300 ohms**. (E9C07) This antenna was very popular when 300 Ω twinlead was used for TV antennas. The reason for this is that 300 Ω was widely available and you could use it for both the antenna and the feedline.

Another popular variation on the half-wave dipole is the off-center fed dipole, or OCFD. An OCFD antenna is **a dipole fed approximately 1/3 the way from one end with a 4:1 balun to provide multiband operation**. (E9C05) The reason this antenna has become so popular is that it not only provides a good match on its fundamental frequency, but on harmonically-related frequencies as well. An OCFD antenna cut for the 80 m band, for example, will also present a good match on 40 m, 15 m, and 10 m bands.

Zepp antennas are also half-wavelength antennas. A Zepp antenna is **an end fed dipole antenna**. (E9C10) Because the impedance is very high at the feedpoint, the Zepp antenna uses a quarter-wave length of transmission line to transform the impedance to something closer to the 50 Ω transmitter output impedance. An extended double Zepp antenna is **a center-fed 1.25 wavelength antenna (two 5/8 wave elements in phase**. (E9C12)

An example of a wire antenna that is not a half-wavelength long is the G5RV antenna. A G5RV antenna is **a multi-band dipole antenna fed with coax and a balun through a selected length of open wire transmission line**. (E9C09) The G5RV was originally designed as a single-band, 20m antenna that provided some directionality. Amateurs soon found that they could easily tune this antenna on other frequency bands, and this multi-band capability has made it very popular.

Rhombic antennas are large wire antennas that have four sections, each one or more wavelengths long, arranged in a rhombic shape, and fed at one end of the rhomboid. When the end opposite the feedpoint is open, the antenna is bidirectional. Putting a terminating resistor on a rhombic antenna, however, **changes the radiation pattern from bidirectional to unidirectional**. (E9C06)

E9D - Directional antennas: gain; Yagi antennas; losses; SWR bandwidth; antenna efficiency; shortened and mobile antennas; RF grounding

This section consists of a miscellaneous selection of antenna questions. We'll start with some questions about directional antennas, then talk a little bit about vertical antennas, then mobile antennas, and finally grounding.

Directional antennas

When designing a Yagi antenna, you might think that the most important parameter is forward gain. What usually occurs if a Yagi antenna is designed solely for maximum forward gain, though, is that **the front-to-back ratio decreases**. (E9D13) In other words, the antenna becomes more bi-directional than simply directional.

On the VHF and UHF bands, Yagi antennas are operated either horizontally for weak-signal work and vertically for FM operations. In some cases, such as operating satellites, circular polarization is desirable. You can use linearly polarized Yagi antennas to produce circular polarization if you **arrange two Yagis perpendicular to each other with the driven elements at the same point on the boom and feed them 90 degrees out of phase**. (E9D02) The disadvantage to this approach is, obviously, that you need two antennas, instead of just one to achieve circular polarization.

Parabolic antennas are often used at microwave frequencies to direct a signal in a particular direction. One thing to keep in mind is that **gain increases by 6 dB** if you are using an ideal parabolic dish antenna when the operating frequency is doubled. (E9D01) Also keep in mind that, as pointed out earlier, the beamwidth is narrower as well.

Antenna efficiency, shortened and mobile antennas

Designing an efficient mobile HF antenna is perhaps the toughest job for a radio amateur. Mobile antennas, almost by definition, must be shorter than a quarter wave and present a capacitive load. What happens to the feed point impedance at the base of a fixed length HF mobile antenna as the frequency of operation is lowered is that **the radiation resistance decreases and the capacitive reactance increases**. (E9D10)

The function of a loading coil as used with an HF mobile antenna is, therefore, **to cancel capacitive reactance**. (E9D09) In effect, loading coils to make the radiator of a short vertical antenna look electrically longer.

Because short verticals have a low radiation resistance, they are inherently inefficient, and you need to do whatever you can to make them as efficient as possible. An HF mobile antenna loading coil should have a high ratio of reactance to resistance **to minimize losses**. (E9D04) A high-Q loading coil (one with a high ratio of reactance to resistance) should be placed **near the center of the vertical radiator** to minimize losses in a shortened vertical antenna. (E9D03)

Unfortunately, what happens to the bandwidth of an antenna as it is shortened through the use of loading coils is that **it is decreased**. (E9D06) In other words, what happens as the Q of an antenna increases is that the **SWR bandwidth decreases**. (E9D08)

One way to improve the efficiency of a short vertical is to use a technique called top loading. An advantage of using top loading in a shortened HF vertical antenna is **improved radiation efficiency**. (E9D07) This is most often accomplished by using a "capacitance hat" on the top of the vertical element.

Often, antennas use traps to yield multi-band operation. A disadvantage of using a multiband trapped antenna is that **it might radiate harmonics**. (E9D05) For example, if your 40m transmissions have high harmonic content on 20m, and the multiband vertical is also resonant on 20m, it will radiate those harmonics.

RF grounding

Much has been written about station grounding. One thing's for sure. A station's safety ground is not adequate as an RF ground. The reason for this is that conductors present different impedances at different frequencies.

A wide flat copper strap is the type of conductor that would be best for minimizing losses in a station's RF ground system. (E9D11)

The main reason for this is that RF tends to be conducted near the surface of a conductor. The more surface area there is, the lower the impedance to ground.

To minimize inductance, it's best to keep the RF ground connection as short as possible. **An electrically-short connection to 3 or 4 interconnected ground rods driven into the Earth** would provide the best RF ground for your station. (E9D12)

E9E - Matching: matching antennas to feed lines; power dividers

For many types of antennas, matching the impedance of the antenna to the impedance of the feedline, normally coax, is essential. Mismatched lines create high SWR and, consequently, feedline losses. **An SWR greater than 1:1** is characteristic of a mismatched transmission line. (E9E08)

When a feedline and antenna are mismatched, some of the power you are trying to transmit will be reflected back down the feedline. The ratio of the amplitude of the reflected wave to the amplitude of the incident wave, or the waver that you're transmitting, is called the reflection coefficient, and it is mathematically related to SWR. **Reflection coefficient** is the term that best describes the interactions at the load end of a mismatched transmission line. (E9E07)

To match the impedance of the feedline to the impedance of the antenna, we use a variety of different techniques. **The delta matching system** matches a high-impedance transmission line to a lower impedance antenna by connecting the line to the driven element in two places spaced a fraction of a wavelength each side of element center. (E9E01)

The gamma match is the name of an antenna matching system that matches an unbalanced feed line to an antenna by feeding the driven element both at the center of the element and at a fraction of a wavelength to one side of center. (E9E02) The purpose of the series capacitor in a gamma-type antenna matching network is **to cancel the inductive reactance of the matching network**. (E9E04)The **gamma match** is an effective method of connecting a 50-ohm coaxial cable feed line to a grounded tower so it can be used as a vertical antenna. (E9E09)

The stub match is the name of the matching system that uses a section of transmission line connected in parallel with the feed line at or near the feed point. (E9E03) What the stub does is to add reactance at the feed point. By varying the length of the stub, you can change the reactance that the stub provides to whatever value is needed. An effective way of matching a feed line to a VHF or UHF antenna when the impedances of both the antenna and feed line are unknown is to **use the universal stub matching technique**. (E9E11)

Inserting a 1/4-wavelength piece of 75-ohm coaxial cable transmission line in series between the antenna terminals and the 50-ohm feed cable is an effective way to match an antenna with a 100-ohm feed point impedance to a 50-ohm coaxial cable feed line. (E9E10) Note that this only works on one band as the length of 75-ohm coax you use will only be 1/4 of a wavelength on one band.

Many directly-fed Yagi antennas have feedpoint impedances of approximately 20 to 25 ohms. One technique often use to match these antennas to 50-ohm coaxial cable is the hairpin match. To use a hairpin matching system to tune the driven element of a 3-element Yagi, **the driven element reactance must be capacitive**. (E9E05) The equivalent lumped-constant network for a hairpin matching system on a 3-element Yagi is **a shunt inductor**. (E9E06)

Some beam antennas use multiple driven elements in order to make them multi-band antennas. The primary purpose of a phasing line when used with an antenna having multiple driven elements is that **it ensures that each driven element operates in concert with the others to create the desired antenna pattern**. (E9E12)

I'm not sure that Wilkinson dividers are used much in antenna systems, or why this question is in the section on feedline matching, but here it is. One use of a Wilkinson divider is that **It is used to divide power equally between two 50 ohm loads while maintaining 50 ohm input impedance**. (E9E13)

E9F - Transmission lines: characteristics of open and shorted feed lines; 1/8 wavelength; 1/4 wavelength; 1/2 wavelength; feed lines: coax versus open-wire; velocity factor; electrical length; coaxial cable dielectrics; velocity factor

The physical length of a coaxial cable transmission line is shorter than its electrical length because **electrical signals move more slowly in a coaxial cable than in air.** (E9F03) The term we use to quantify the difference in how fast a wave travels in air versus how fast it travels in a feedline is velocity factor.

The velocity factor of a transmission line is **the velocity of the wave in the transmission line divided by the velocity of light in a vacuum.** (E9F01) Put another way, **velocity factor** is the term for the ratio of the actual speed at which a signal travels through a transmission line to the speed of light in a vacuum. (E9F08) **The dielectric materials used in the line** determines the velocity factor of a transmission line. (E9F02)

The typical velocity factor for a coaxial cable with solid polyethylene dielectric is **0.66.** (E9F04) That makes the approximate physical length of a solid polyethylene dielectric coaxial transmission line that is electrically one-quarter wavelength long at 14.1 MHz about **3.5 meters.** (E9F05) The approximate physical length of a solid polyethylene dielectric coaxial transmission line that is electrically one-quarter wavelength long at 7.2 MHz is **6.9 meters.** (E9F09)

The velocity factor of air-insulated, parallel conductor transmission lines is a lot closer to 1 than the velocity factor for coaxial cable. The approximate physical length of an air-insulated, parallel conductor transmission line that is electrically one-half wavelength long at 14.10 MHz is **10 meters.** (E9F06)

While having a higher velocity factor is not really such a big advantage, open-wire or ladder line feedlines do have other advantages. For example, ladder line has **lower loss** than small-diameter coaxial cable such as RG-58 at 50 MHz. (E9F07)

Sometimes we use various lengths of coax to match an antenna system or to filter out frequencies. A 1/8-wavelength transmission line presents **an inductive reactance** to a generator when the line is shorted at the far end. (E9F10) A 1/8-wavelength transmission line presents **a capacitive reactance** to a generator when the line is open at the far end. (E9F11)

A 1/4-wavelength transmission line presents **a very low impedance** to a generator when the line is open at the far end. (E9F12) A 1/4-wavelength transmission line presents a **very high impedance** to a generator when the line is shorted at the far end. (E9F13)

A 1/2-wavelength transmission line presents a **very low impedance** to a generator when the line is shorted at the far end. (E9F14) A 1/2-wavelength transmission line presents a **very high impedance** to a generator when the line is open at the far end. (E9F15)

All of these choices are correct when talking about significant differences between foam-dielectric coaxial cable and solid-dielectric cable, assuming all other parameters are the same (E9F16):

- Foam dielectric has lower safe operating voltage limits
- Foam dielectric has lower loss per unit of length
- Foam dielectric has higher velocity factor

E9G - The Smith chart

Figure E9-3

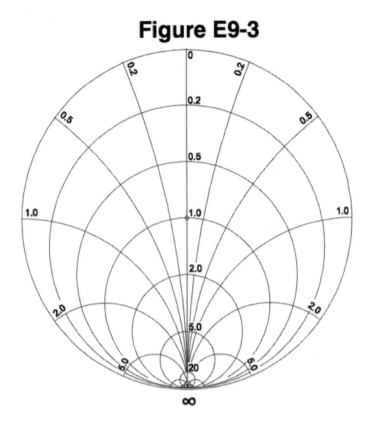

A **Smith chart** is shown in Figure E9-3 above. (E9G05) It is a chart designed to solve transmission line problems graphically. While a complete discussion of the theory behind the Smith Chart is outside the scope of this study guide, a good discussion of the Smith Chart can be found on the ARRL website (http://www.arrl.org/files/file/ Antenna%20Book%20Supplemental%20Files/22nd%20Edition/ Smith%20Chart%20Supplement%20-%20Corrected%20Jan %202012.pdf).

The coordinate system is used in a Smith chart is comprised of **resistance circles and reactance arcs**. (E9G02) **Resistance and reactance** are the two families of circles and arcs that make up a Smith chart. (E9G04)

The resistance axis is the only straight line shown on the Smith chart shown in Figure E9-3. (E9G07) Points on this axis are pure resistances. In practice, you want to position the chart so that 0 ohms is at the far left, while infinity is at the far right.

The arcs on a Smith chart represent **points with constant reactance**. (E9G10) On the Smith chart, shown in Figure E9-3, the name for the large outer circle on which the reactance arcs terminate is the **reactance axis**. (E9G06) Points on the reactance axis have a resistance of 0 ohms. When oriented so that the resistance axis is horizontal, positive reactances are plotted above the resistance axis and negative reactances below.

The process of normalization with regard to a Smith chart refers to **reassigning impedance values with regard to the prime center**. (E9G08) The prime center is the point marked 1.0 on the resistance axis. If you're working with a 50 ohm transmission line, you'd normally divide the impedances by 50, meaning that a 50 ohm resistance would then be plotted on the resistance axis at the point marked 1.0. A reactance of 50 + j100 would be plotted on the resistance circle going through the prime center where it intersects the reactance arc marked 2.0.

Impedance along transmission lines can be calculated using a Smith chart. (E9G01) **Impedance and SWR values in transmission lines** are often determined using a Smith chart. (E9G03) **Standing-wave ratio circles** are often added to a Smith chart during the process of solving problems. (E9G09)

The wavelength scales on a Smith chart are calibrated **in fractions of transmission line electrical wavelength**. (E9G11) These are useful when trying to determine how long transmission lines must be when used to match a load to a transmitter.

E9H - Receiving Antennas: radio direction finding antennas; Beverage Antennas; specialized receiving antennas; longwire receiving antennas

Many antennas, such as the Beverage antenna, are designed to be receiving antennas only. When constructing a Beverage antenna, one of the factors that should be included in the design is that **it should be one or more wavelengths long** to achieve good performance at the desired frequency. (E9H01)

While directionality is a desirable feature for a receiving antenna, gain often is not, especially on the low bands. The reason for this is that **atmospheric noise is so high that gain over a dipole is not important** for low band (160 meter and 80 meter) receiving antennas. (E9H02)

Direction finding antennas

Direction finding is an activity that's both fun and useful. One of the ways that it's useful is to hunt down noise sources. It can also be used to hunt down stations causing harmful interference.

A variety of directional antennas are used in direction finding, including the shielded loop antenna. A receiving loop antenna consists of **one or more turns of wire wound in the shape of a large open coil**. (E9H09) The output voltage of a multi-turn receiving loop antenna can be increased **by increasing either the number of wire turns in the loop or the area of the loop structure or both**. (E9H10)

An advantage of using a shielded loop antenna for direction finding is that **it is electro-statically balanced against ground, giving better nulls**. (E9H04) The main drawback of a wire-loop antenna for direction finding is that **it has a bidirectional pattern**. (E9H05)

Sometimes a sense antenna is used with a direction finding antenna. The function of a sense antenna is that **it modifies the pattern of a DF antenna array to provide a null in one direction**. (E9H08)

Another way to obtain a null in only one direction is to build an antenna array with a cardioid pattern. One way to do this is to build an array with two dipoles fed in quadrature. **A very sharp single null** is a characteristic of a cardioid-pattern antenna that is useful for direction finding. (E9H11)

Another accessory that is often used in direction finding is an attenuator. It is advisable to use an RF attenuator on a receiver being used for direction finding because **it prevents receiver overload which could make it difficult to determine peaks or nulls**. (E9H07)

If more than one operator can be mobilized for a direction-finding operation, they could use the triangulation method for finding a noise source or the source of a radio signal. When using the triangulation method of direction finding, **antenna headings from several different receiving locations are used to locate the signal source**. (E9H06)

E3: RADIO WAVE PROPAGATION

E3A - Electromagnetic waves; Earth-Moon-Earth communications; meteor scatter; microwave tropospheric and scatter propagation; aurora propagation

An electromagnetic wave is **a wave consisting of an electric field and a magnetic field oscillating at right angles to each other**. (E3A15) Electromagnetic waves travel in free space because **changing electric and magnetic fields propagate the energy**. (E3A16)

An important characteristic of an electromagnetic wave is its polarization. A wave is said to be vertically polarized if its electric field is perpendicular to the Earth and horizontally polarized if the electric field is parallel to the Earth. **Waves with a rotating electric field** are circularly polarized electromagnetic waves. (E3A17)

Moon bounce, or Earth-Moon-Earth (EME) communication

One of the more exotic amateur radio activities is earth-moon-earth (EME) communication, sometimes called "moon bounce." As this name implies, radio amateurs actually bounce their signals off the moon. This is the ultimate DX. The approximate maximum separation measured along the surface of the Earth between two stations communicating by Moon bounce is **12,000 miles, if the**

Moon is visible by both. (E3A01)

Because the signal travels such a long way, you need to do everything you can to avoid signal loss. So, for example, scheduling EME contacts **when the Moon is at perigee** will generally result in the least path loss. (E3A03) Perigee is the point at which the Moon is the closest to Earth.

One interesting phenomenon is libration fading. Libration fading of an Earth-Moon-Earth signal is **a fluttery, irregular fading**. (E3A02) This fading is caused by the irregular surface of the Moon, and the peaks can last for up to two seconds on the 2m band. These peaks can actually help operators make contacts when they would otherwise be impossible.

Meteor scatter

Some amateur radio operators bounce their signals off meteor trails. This type of propagation is called meteor scatter. Meteor scatter propagation is possible because when a meteor strikes the Earth's atmosphere, a cylindrical region of free electrons is formed at **the E layer** of the ionosphere. (E3A08) **28 - 148 MHz** is the frequency range that is well suited for meteor-scatter communications. (E3A09)

Microwave tropospheric and scatter propagation

While HF propagation is not affected by weather conditions, the same cannot be said for microwave propagation. **Temperature inversion** is the type of atmospheric structure can create a path for microwave propagation. (E3A10) These paths form in the troposphere and and are often called tropospheric ducts.

Tropospheric propagation of microwave signals often occurs along **warm and cold fronts**. (E3A05) And, atmospheric ducts capable of propagating microwave signals often form over **bodies of water**. (E3A07) The typical range for tropospheric propagation of microwave signals is **1200 miles**. (E3A11)

Tropospheric propagation is quite predictable. There are even websites that you can visit that will tell you where tropospheric ducts currently exist. These websites include William Hepburn's Radio & TV DX Information Centre (http://www.dxinfocentre.com/tropo.

html). This site shows where ducting is occurring on Hepburn maps, which are maps that predict the **probability of tropospheric propagation**. (E3A04)

Rain can also affect the propagation of microwave signals. **The rain must be within radio range of both stations** for microwave propagation via rain scatter. (E3A06)

Aurora propagation

Another interesting type of propagation is aurora propagation. The cause of auroral activity—sometimes called the Northern Lights—is **the interaction in the E layer of charged particles from the Sun with the Earth's magnetic field**. (E3A12)

From the contiguous 48 states, **North** is the approximate direction an antenna should be pointed to take maximum advantage of aurora propagation. (E3A14) **CW** is the emission mode that is best for aurora propagation. (E3A13)

E3B - Transequatorial propagation; long path; gray-line; multi-path; ordinary and extraordinary waves; chordal hop, sporadic E mechanisms

There are a number of interesting types of propagation that occur on the HF bands. They include transequatorial propagation, long-path propagation, and gray-line propagation.

Transequatorial propagation is **propagation between two mid-latitude points at approximately the same distance north and south of the magnetic equator.** (E3B01) The approximate maximum range for signals using transequatorial propagation is **5000 miles.** (E3B02) The best time of day for transequatorial propagation is **afternoon or early evening.** (E3B03)

Long-path propagation is the type of propagation that occurs when the longer of the two direct paths between stations is better for communications than the shorter path. **160 to 10 meters** are the amateur bands that typically support long-path propagation. (E3B05) **20 meters** is the amateur band that most frequently provides long-path propagation. (E3B06)

Gray-line is the type of HF propagation that is probably occurring if radio signals travel along the terminator between daylight and darkness. (E3B08) Gray-line propagation occurs because, **at twilight, D-layer absorption drops while E-layer and F-layer propagation remain strong.** (E3B10)

Another interesting propagation phenomenon is echoes. While not strictly a type of propagation, echoes are the result of propagation conditions. **Receipt of a signal by more than one path** is one condition that could account for hearing an echo on the received signal of a distant station. (E3B07)

Sporadic-E propagation occurs when unusally dense patches of ionization form in the E layer of the ionosphere. The time of year that Sporadic E propagation is most likely to occur is **around the solstices, especially the summer solstice.** (E3B09) Sporadic-E propagation is most likely to occur **any time** of the day. (E3B11)

Chordal hop propagation occurs when a radio wave is refracted by the ionosphere such that the refracted wave hits the ionosphere again before hitting the ground. The primary characteristic of chordal hop propagation is **successive ionospheric reflections without an intermediate reflection from the ground**. (E3B12) Chordal hop propagation is desirable because **the signal experiences less loss along the path compared to normal skip propagation**. (E3B13)

When a radio wave enters the ionosphere, it splits into two waves called the ordinary wave and the extraordinary wave. The terms extraordinary and ordinary waves describe **independent waves created in the ionosphere that are elliptically polarized**. (E3B04) What happens to linearly polarized radio waves that split into ordinary and extraordinary waves in the ionosphere is that **they become elliptically polarized**. (E3B14)

E3C - Radio-path horizon; less common propagation modes; propagation prediction techniques and modeling; space weather parameters and amateur radio

While we say that VHF/UHF communication is "line of sight," the distance that a VHF/UHF radio wave will travel is slightly longer than the line-of-sight distance. We call this distance the "radio horizon" or "radio-path horizon." The VHF/UHF radio-path horizon distance exceeds the geometric horizon **by approximately 15% of the distance**. (E3C06) The radio-path horizon distance exceeds the geometric horizon because of **downward bending due to density variations in the atmosphere**. (E3C14)

Amateur radio operators may sometimes use ground-wave propagation to communicate. One important thing to know about this type of propagation is that the maximum distance of ground-wave propagation **decreases** when the signal frequency is increased. (E3C12) **Vertical** polarization is the best type of polarization for ground-wave propagation. (E3C13) So, if you really want to make a contact via ground wave, use a vertical antenna on the 160m band.

Prediction techniques and modeling

Since it's very advantageous to know the propagation conditions for a particular signal path, many hams use propagation prediction software to choose what frequency bands to use. One of these software packages is called VOACAP, because it was developed by engineers at the Voice of America (VOA). VOACAP software models **HF propagation**. (E3C11)

Often, these types of software packages use a technique called ray tracing. In regard to radio communications, the term ray tracing describes the process of **modeling a radio wave's path through the ionosphere**. (E3C01)

Propagation prediction software uses data such as the A index and K index to model propagation. Both of these provide a measure of geomagnetic activity, which affects HF propagation. A rising A or K index indicates **increasing disruption of the geomagnetic field**.

(E3C02) A high A-index or K-index usually means that HF propagation will be poor. **Polar paths** are most likely to experience high levels of absorption when the A index or K index is elevated. (E3C03)

The interplanetary magnetic field has a very strong affect on HF propagation. The value of Bz (B sub Z) represents **the direction and strength of the interplanetary magnetic field**. (E3C04) A **southward** orientation of Bz (B sub z) increases the likelihood that incoming particles from the Sun will cause disturbed conditions. (E3C05) HF propagation is generally poor when Bz is oriented southward and geomagnetic conditions are disturbed.

Space weather parameters and amateur radio

Because solar radiation creates the ionosphere, solar activity has a great impact on radio wave propations. These conditions are often referred to as space weather.

Solar flares, for example, emit an enormous amount of radiation. Depending on how much radiation they emit, the effect on HF propagation can be good or bad. If the Earth receives only enough radiation to increase ionization in the upper layers of the ionosphere, HF propagation is improved.

If the level of radiation is higher, the lower levels of the ionosphere could become more energized. When this happens, they absorb more RF energy, and HF propagation is poor. A sudden rise in radio background noise indicates that **a solar flare has occurred**. (E3C15)

Solar flares are categorized by intensity. Class A solar flares are the least intense. **Class X** is the descriptor that indicates the greatest solar flare intensity. (E3C07) In between Class A and Class X are Class B, Class C, and Class M.

Within each class, solar flares are assigned a value from 1 – 9. The intensity of an X3 flare is **twice as great** as that of an X2 flare. (E3C09)

The National Oceanic and Atmospheric Administration (NOAA) has developed what they call Space Weather Scales to communicate to the general public the current and future space weather conditions and their possible effects on people and systems. The G scale indicates geomagnetic conditions. The space weather term G5 means **an extreme geomagnetic storm**. (E3C08)

Sunspots are often used to predict HF propagation conditions. The more sunspots, the better HF propagation is. Paramater 304a may, however, be an even better indicator of radio conditions. The 304A solar parameter measures **UV emissions at 304 angstroms, correlated to solar flux index**. (E3C10) These UV emissions are one of the principle causes of F2 layer ionization.

E4: AMATEUR PRACTICES

E4A - Test equipment: analog and digital instruments; spectrum and network analyzers, antenna analyzers; oscilloscopes; RF measurements; computer aided measurements

An instrument that amateur radio operators frequently use when experimenting or when debugging equipment is the oscilloscope, or simply just "scope." Oscilloscopes have become more common in amateur radio shacks as prices have fallen, and the technology has moved from analog to digital.

Analog oscilloscopes use amplifiers, filters, and other analog signal processing circuits to display an input signal on a cathode-ray tube, or CRT. Digital oscilloscopes, on the other hand, use an analog-to-digital converter to convert the input signal into a series of numbers, which are then processed by a computer and displayed on an LCD screen. **All of these choices are correct** when talking about the advantages of a digital vs. analog oscilloscope: (E4A05)
- Automatic amplitude and frequency numerical readout
- Storage of traces for future reference
- Manipulation of time base after trace capture

One of the most important oscilloscope specifications is its bandwidth. The bandwidth of an oscilloscope determines the maximum frequency at which the oscilloscope can accurately measure a signal. While the characteristics of the analog signal processing circuits determine the bandwidth of an analog oscilloscope, **sampling rate** is the parameter that determines the bandwidth of a digital or computer-based oscilloscope. (E4A01) Similarly, the **analog-to-digital conversion speed of the soundcard** determines the upper frequency limit for a computer soundcard-based oscilloscope program. (E4A04)

Because digital oscilloscopes sample an input signal at discrete time intervals, it is possible to fool them into displaying an incorrect waveform. This phenomenon is called aliasing. The effect of aliasing in a digital or computer-based oscilloscope is that **false signals are displayed**. (E4A06) When using a computer's soundcard input to digitize signals, the highest frequency signal that can be digitized without aliasing is **one-half the sample rate**. (E4A09)

Oscilloscope probes

When making measurements at RF frequencies, it's important to connect the probe's ground connection as close to the location of the measurement as possible. **Keeping the signal ground connection of the probe as short as possible** is good practice when using an oscilloscope probe. (E4A11) Keeping this connection as short as possible reduces the noise picked up by the probe and reduces the inductance of the connection, which in turn, makes the measurement more accurate.

Good quality passive oscilloscope probes have an adjustable capacitor in them that needs to be adjusted so that the probe capacitive reactance is at least nine times the scope input capacitive reactance. When this capacitor is adjusted properly, we say that the probe is properly compensated, and the scope will display the waveform with as little distortion as possible.

How is the compensation of an oscilloscope probe typically adjusted? **A square wave is displayed and the probe is adjusted until the horizontal portions of the displayed wave are as nearly flat as possible**. (E4A13) High-quality oscilloscopes will have a special square-wave output specifically for the purpose of compensating probes.

Spectrum analyzers

Spectrum analyzers display the amplitude of signals in the frequency domain. **Frequency** is the parameter a spectrum analyzer would display on the horizontal axis. (E4A02) The drawing below shows typical displays from an oscilloscope and a spectrum analyzer. Spectrum analyzers are very useful for troubleshooting problems. For example, **a spectrum analyzer** is used to display spurious signals from a radio transmitter. (E4A03)

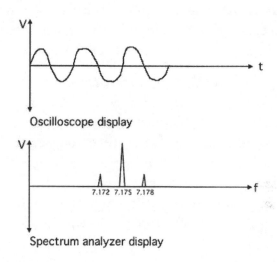

Because spectrum analyzers are sensitive instruments, you need to be cautious when using them. For example, an important precaution to follow when connecting a spectrum analyzer to a transmitter output is to **attenuate the transmitter output going to the spectrum analyzer**. (E4A12) Not doing so could damage the spectrum analyzer because its input circuits are not designed to handle high power.

Antenna analyzers

One of the instruments that I think every amateur radio operator should have (or at least have access to) is the antenna analyzer. Antenna analyzers are versatile instruments that allow amateur radio operators to easily make antenna measurements, as well as other impedance measurements. They can even be used as low power RF signal generators.

An antenna analyzer is the instrument that would be best for measuring the SWR of a beam antenna. (E4A08) Actually, it's the best instrument for measuring the SWR of any kind of antenna. That's what they're made for! When measuring antenna resonance and feed point impedance with a portable antenna analyzer, **connect the antenna feed line directly to the analyzer's connector.** (E4B11)

An advantage of using an antenna analyzer compared to an SWR bridge to measure antenna SWR is that **antenna analyzers do not need an external RF source.** (E4A07) What this means is that you don't need to connect your transmitter to the antenna to tune it. This is because antenna analyzers have internal RF signal generators.

Frequency counters, logic analyzers

To measure the frequency of a signal, you use an instrument called a frequency counter. When selecting a frequency counter, an important specification is the maximum frequency. If you want to measure the frequency of a signal whose frequency is higher than the maximum frequency of your counter, you might use a prescaler. The purpose of a prescaler function on a frequency counter is to **divide a higher frequency signal so a low-frequency counter can display the input frequency.** (E4A14)

Most frequency counters work by counting the number of cycles of a signal during a given time period. An alternate method of determining frequency used by some counters is period measurement plus mathematical computation. An advantage of a period-measuring frequency counter over a direct-count type is that **it provides improved resolution of low-frequency signals within a comparable time period.** (E4A15)

The proper operation of a digital circuit depends on the output state of many digital ICs at specific times. To ensure that a circuit is working properly, or to troubleshoot a circuit, you may want to use a logic analyzer. A **logic analyzer** displays multiple digital signal states simultaneously. (E4A10)

E4B - Measurement techniques: Instrument accuracy and performance limitations; probes; techniques to minimize errors; measurement of Q; instrument calibration

When making measurements, you should keep in mind that test instruments are not 100% accurate. What that means is that the instrument reading is not exactly the value of the parameter you're measuring. The reading is always going to be off by some amount.

Let's consider frequency counters. Frequency counters are useful instruments for measuring the output frequency of amateur radio transceivers. While a number of different factors can affect the accuracy of an instrument, **time base accuracy** is the factor that most affects the accuracy of a frequency counter. (E4B01) The time base accuracy of most inexpensive frequency counters is about 1 part per million, or 1 ppm.

Now, let's see how that affects the accuracy of a frequency measurement. If a frequency counter with a specified accuracy of +/- 1.0 ppm reads 146,520,000 Hz, **146.52 Hz** is the most the actual frequency being measured could differ from the reading. (E4B03) Practically, what this means is that while the frequency counter reads 146,520,000 Hz, or 146.52 MHz, the actual frequency of the signal might be as low as 146.519853 MHz or as high as 146.520147 MHz.

More accurate—and therefore more expensive—frequency counters might have a specified accuracy of 0.1 ppm. If a frequency counter with a specified accuracy of +/- 0.1 ppm reads 146,520,000 Hz, **14.652 Hz** is the most the actual frequency being measured could differ from the reading. (E4B04) This is very accurate for amateur radio work.

Very inexpensive frequency counters might have an accuracy of only 10 ppm. If a frequency counter with a specified accuracy of +/- 10 ppm reads 146,520,000 Hz, **1465.20 Hz** is the most the actual frequency being measured could differ from the reading. (E4B05) This might be adequate for amateur radio work, but as you can see, the difference between the frequency counter's reading and the signal's actual frequency can be up to ten times as much as with the frequency counter with a 1 ppm accuracy.

Voltmeters

Probably the most common test instrument in an amateur radio station is a voltmeter. The voltmeter may be part of a digital multimeter (DMM) or volt-ohm meter (VOM). DMMs have the advantage of high input impedance, and **high impedance input** is a characteristic of a good DC voltmeter. (E4B08) The higher the input impedance, the less effect the meter will have on the measurement.

The input impedance of a VOM is calculated using the VOM's sensitivity expressed in ohms per volt. **The full scale reading of the voltmeter multiplied by its ohms per volt rating will provide the input impedance of the voltmeter.** (E4B12) A higher ohms per volt rating means that it will have a higher input impedance than a meter with a lower ohms per volt rating.

RF measurements

Directional power meters and RF ammeters are two instruments that you can use to make antenna measurements. With a directional power meter, you could measure the forward power and reflected power and then figure out how much power is being delivered to the load and calculate the SWR of the antenna system. For example, **75 watts** is the power is being absorbed by the load when a directional power meter connected between a transmitter and a terminating load reads 100 watts forward power and 25 watts reflected power. (E4B06)

With an RF ammeter, you measure the RF current flowing in the antenna system. If the current reading on an RF ammeter placed in series with the antenna feed line of a transmitter increases as the transmitter is tuned to resonance it means **there is more power going into the antenna.** (E4B09)

There are a number of instruments that you can use to measure the impedance of a circuit. An antenna analyzer is one. An instrument with a bridge circuit, such as a noise bridge, is another. An advantage of using an instrument with a bridge circuit to measure impedance is that **the measurement is based on obtaining a signal null, which can be done very precisely**. (E4B02)

Other instruments, such as the dip meter, also use this principle. You adjust a dip meter's controls so that the reading "dips" to a minimum value. The control settings then indicate the resonant frequency. When using a dip meter, don't couple it too tightly to the circuit under test. **A less accurate reading results** if a dip meter is too tightly coupled to a tuned circuit being checked. (E4B14)

For some experiments, you'll want to know not only the resonant frequency of a circuit but also the quality factor, or Q, of the circuit. **The bandwidth of the circuit's frequency response** can be used as a relative measurement of the Q for a series-tuned circuit. (E4B15)

Another type of instrument that you can use to make impedance measurements is the vector network analyzer. As with any instrument, you need to ensure that it is calibrated properly. Three test loads used to calibrate a standard RF vector network analyzer are **short circuit, open circuit, and 50 ohms**. (E4B17)

Finally, a method to measure intermodulation distortion in an SSB transmitter is to **modulate the transmitter with two non-harmonically related audio frequencies and observe the RF output with a spectrum analyzer**. (E4B10) The instrument we use to do this is called, oddly enough, a two-tone generator. Typically, these generators provide tones of 700 Hz and 1,900 Hz simultaneously.

S parameters

S-parameters, or scattering parameters, are used to describe the behavior of RF devices under linear conditions. Each parameter is typically characterized by magnitude, decibel and phase.

The subscripts of S parameters represent **the port or ports at which measurements are made**. (E4B07) The S parameter that is equivalent to forward gain is **S21**. (E4B13) The S parameter that represents return loss or SWR is **S11**. (E4B16)

E4C - Receiver performance characteristics, phase noise, noise floor, image rejection, MDS, signal-to-noise-ratio; selectivity; effects of SDR receiver non-linearity

In the past, sensitivity was one of the most important receiver performance specifications. Today, instead of sensitivity, we speak of a receiver's minimum discernible signal, or MDS. The MDS of a receiver is **the minimum discernible signal**. (E4C07) This is the weakest signal that a receiver will detect. One parameter that affects a receiver's MDS is the noise figure. The noise figure of a receiver is **the ratio in dB of the noise generated by the receiver compared to the theoretical minimum noise**. (E4C04)

A related specification is the noise floor. When we say that the noise floor of a receiver has a value of -174 dBm/Hz, it is referring to **the theoretical noise at the input of a perfect receiver at room temperature**. (E4C05) If a CW receiver with the AGC off has an equivalent input noise power density of -174 dBm/Hz, the level of an unmodulated carrier input to this receiver would have to be **-148 dBm** to yield an audio output SNR of 0 dB in a 400 Hz noise bandwidth. (E4C06)

Another important receiver specification is selectivity. A receiver's selectivity is the result of a lot of things, including the filters a receiver has. **300 Hz** is a desirable amount of selectivity for an amateur RTTY HF receiver. (E4C10) **2.4 kHz** is a desirable amount of selectivity for an amateur SSB phone receiver. (E4C11)

In addition to a 300 Hz filter and a 2.4 kHz filter, high-end receivers also have filters called roofing filters. A narrow-band roofing filter affects receiver performance because **it improves dynamic range by attenuating strong signals near the receive frequency**. (E4C13)

Back in the day, when superheterodyne receivers had intermediate frequencies, or IFs, in the 400 - 500 kHz range, image rejection was a problem. If there was a strong signal present on a frequency about two times the IF away from the frequency your receiver was tuned to, you might hear that signal. Accordingly, **15.210 MHz** is a frequency on which a station might be transmitting if it is generating a spurious image signal in a receiver tuned to 14.300 MHz and which uses a 455 kHz IF frequency. (E4C14)

One solution to this problem is to select a higher IF frequency. One good reason for selecting a high frequency for the design of the IF in a conventional HF or VHF communications receiver is that it is **easier for front-end circuitry to eliminate image responses**. (E4C09) **A front-end filter or pre-selector** of a receiver can also be effective in eliminating image signal interference. (E4C02)

Another way to get rid of image signals is to use a narrow IF filter. An undesirable effect of using too wide a filter bandwidth in the IF section of a receiver is that **undesired signals may be heard**. (E4C12)

Because most modern transceivers use digital techniques to generate a local oscillator signal to tune a receiver, synthesizer phase noise might be a problem. An effect of excessive phase noise in the local oscillator section of a receiver is that **it can cause strong signals on nearby frequencies to interfere with reception of weak signals**. (E4C01)

Software-defined radio (SDR) is becoming more popular in amateur radio. It is, therefore, necessary to know something about SDR receiver characteristics. The SDR receiver's **analog-to-digital converter sample width in bits** has the largest effect on an SDR receiver's linearity. (E4C17) An SDR receiver is overloaded when input signals exceeds **the maximum count value of the analog-to-digital converter**. (E4C08) **Distortion** is caused by missing codes in an SDR receiver's analog-to-digital converter. (E4C16)

Finally, here are two miscellaneous questions on receiver performance characteristics. **Atmospheric noise** is the primary source of noise that can be heard from an HF receiver with an antenna connected. (E4C15) **Capture effect** is the term for the blocking of one FM phone signal by another, stronger FM phone signal. (E4C03)

E4D - Receiver performance characteristics: blocking dynamic range; intermodulation and cross-modulation interference; 3rd order intercept; desensitization; preselector

One of the most commonly mentioned HF receiver specifications is blocking dynamic range. The blocking dynamic range of a receiver is **the difference in dB between the noise floor and the level of an incoming signal which will cause 1 dB of gain compression**. (E4D01) **Cross-modulation of the desired signal and desensitization from strong adjacent signals** are two problems caused by poor dynamic range in a communications receiver. (E4D02)

Another specification commonly bandied about is third-order intercept level. A third-order intercept level of 40 dBm with respect to receiver performance means **a pair of 40 dBm signals will theoretically generate a third-order intermodulation product with the same level as the input signals**. (E4D10) Compared to other products, third-order intermodulation products created within a receiver are of particular interest because **the third-order product of two signals which are in the band of interest is also likely to be within the band**. (E4D11)

The term for the reduction in receiver sensitivity caused by a strong signal near the received frequency is **desensitization**. (E4D12) **Strong adjacent-channel signals** can cause receiver desensitization. (E4D13) One way to reduce the likelihood of receiver desensitization is to **decrease the RF bandwidth of the receiver**. (E4D14)

A preselector might help in some cases. The purpose of the preselector in a communications receiver is **to increase rejection of unwanted signals**. (E4D09)

When operating a repeater, one thing that can occur is intermodulation interference, or simply intermod. **Intermodulation interference** is the term for unwanted signals generated by the mixing of two or more signals. (E4D06) **Nonlinear circuits or devices** cause intermodulation in an electronic circuit. (E4D08)

Intermodulation interference between two repeaters occurs **when** the repeaters are in close proximity and the signals mix in the final amplifier of one or both transmitters. (E4D03) The transmitter frequencies would cause an intermodulation-product signal in a receiver tuned to 146.70 MHz when a nearby station transmits on 146.52 MHz are **146.34 MHz and 146.61 MHz.** (E4D05) We get this in the following way:

2 x 146.52 MHz - 146.34 MHz = 146.70 MHz and

2 x 146.61 MHz - 146.52 MHz = 146.70 MHz

A properly terminated circulator at the output of the transmitter may reduce or eliminate intermodulation interference in a repeater caused by another transmitter operating in close proximity. (E4D04) The circulator reduces intermodulation distortion because it helps to reduce the amount of energy from nearby transmitters that might get into a repeater's final amplifier.

Cross modulation is a form of intermodulation. Cross modulation occurs when a very strong signal combines with a weaker signal and actually modulates the weaker signal. The most significant effect of an off-frequency signal when it is causing cross-modulation interference to a desired signal is that **the off-frequency unwanted signal is heard in addition to the desired signal.** (E4D07)

E4E - Noise suppression: system noise; electrical appliance noise; line noise; locating noise sources; DSP noise reduction; noise blankers; grounding for signals

Noise is often a real problem for radio amateurs. Fortunately, by understanding how noise is generated and how to reduce or eliminate it, noise can be tamed.

Atmospheric noise is naturally-occurring noise. **Thunderstorms are a major cause of atmospheric static.** (E4E06) There's not much you can do to eliminate atmospheric noise, but you can often use a receiver's noise blanker to help you copy signals better. **Signals which appear across a wide bandwidth** (like atmospheric noise) are the types of signals that a receiver noise blanker might be able to remove from desired signals. (E4E03) **Ignition noise** is one type of receiver noise that can often be reduced by use of a receiver noise blanker. (E4E01)

One undesirable effect that can occur when using a receiver's IF noise blanker is that **nearby signals may appear to be excessively wide even if they meet emission standards.** (E4E09)

Many modern receivers now use digital signal processing (DSP) filters to eliminate noise. **All of these choices are correct** when talking about types of receiver noise that can often be reduced with a DSP noise filter (E4E02):

- Broadband white noise
- Ignition noise
- Power line noise

One disadvantage of using some types of automatic DSP notch-filters when attempting to copy CW signals is that **the DSP filter can remove the desired signal at the same time as it removes interfering signals.** (E4E12)

While filters can be very effective at reducing noise, it is often better to figure out what is generating the noise and take steps to reduce or eliminate the amount of noise generated in the first place. For example, one way you can determine if line noise interference is being generated within your home is **by turning off the AC power line main circuit breaker and listening on a battery operated radio**. (E4E07) If by doing this you determine that an electric motor is a problem, noise from an electric motor can be suppressed **by installing a brute-force AC-line filter in series with the motor leads**. (E4E05)

All of these choices are correct when it comes to the cause of a loud roaring or buzzing AC line interference that comes and goes at intervals (E4E13):

- Arcing contacts in a thermostatically controlled device
- A defective doorbell or doorbell transformer inside a nearby residence
- A malfunctioning illuminated advertising display

Sometimes your own equipment may be the cause of received noise. Cables in an amateur radio station, for example, can radiate or pick up interference. Common mode currents are the culprits. **Common-mode current** flows equally on all conductors of an unshielded multi-conductor cable. (E4E16) **Common mode currents on the shield and conductors** can cause shielded cables to radiate or receive interference. (E4E15) To eliminate this interference, make sure to ground the shield at one end of the cable.

Electrical wiring may also pick up interference. **A common-mode signal at the frequency of the radio transmitter** is sometimes picked up by electrical wiring near a radio antenna. (E4E08)

The main source of noise in an automobile is the alternator. Conducted and radiated noise caused by an automobile alternator can be suppressed **by connecting the radio's power leads directly to the battery and by installing coaxial capacitors in line with the alternator leads**. (E4E04)

Personal computers and other digital devices can also generate noise. One type of electrical interference that might be caused by the operation of a nearby personal computer is **the appearance of unstable modulated or unmodulated signals at specific frequencies**. (E4E14) **All of these choices are correct** when talking about common characteristics of interference caused by a touch controlled electrical device: (E4E10)

- The interfering signal sounds like AC hum on an AM receiver or a carrier modulated by 60 Hz hum on a SSB or CW receiver
- The interfering signal may drift slowly across the HF spectrum
- The interfering signal can be several kHz in width and usually repeats at regular intervals across a HF band

Noise can even be generated by the most unlikely things. For example, it is mostly likely that **nearby corroded metal joints are mixing and re-radiating the broadcast signals** if you are hearing combinations of local AM broadcast signals within one or more of the MF or HF ham bands. (E4E11)

E2: OPERATING PROCEDURES

E2A - Amateur radio in space: amateur satellites; orbital mechanics; frequencies and modes; satellite hardware; satellite operations; experimental telemetry applications

Working satellites is a very popular amateur radio activity. There's even an organization dedicated to launching and operating amateur radio satellites - AMSAT (www.amsat.org).

Perhaps the most important thing you need to know when trying to communicate via satellite is where the satellites are. One way to predict the location of a satellite at a given time is **by calculations using the Keplerian elements for the specified satellite**. (E2A12)

Amateur radio satellites are not in a geostationary orbit. That is to say they are constantly changing position in relationship to a point on the Earth. The type of satellite appears to stay in one position in the sky is **geostationary**. (E2A13)

When determining where a satellite is, you might want to know its orbital period. The orbital period of an Earth satellite is **the time it takes for a satellite to complete one revolution around the Earth**. (E2A03)

It's also important to know the direction in which it is traveling. The direction of an ascending pass for an amateur satellite is **from**

south to north. (E2A01) The direction of a descending pass for an amateur satellite is **from north to south**. (E2A02)

Next, you need to know what mode the satellite is in. The term mode as applied to an amateur radio satellite means **the satellite's uplink and downlink frequency bands**. (E2A04)

We use a combination of letters to denote the mode. The letters in a satellite's mode designator specify **the uplink and downlink frequency ranges**. (E2A05) If it were operating in mode U/V, a satellite's receive signals would be in the **435-438 MHz** band. (E2A06) U stands for UHF, V for VHF. With regard to satellite communications, the terms L band and S band specify **the 23 centimeter and 13 centimeter bands**. (E2A09)

Satellites repeat signals using transponders. Transponders are similar to repeaters, except that they receive signals across a band of frequencies and repeat them across another band of frequencies. The most common type of transponder is the linear transponder. **All of these choices are correct** when talking about the types of signals can be relayed through a linear transponder (E2A07):

- FM and CW
- SSB and SSTV
- PSK and Packet

One thing to keep in mind when operating satellites is to keep your transmitter power to the minimum needed to hit the satellite. Effective radiated power to a satellite which uses a linear transponder should be limited **to avoid reducing the downlink power to all other users**. (E2A08)

There are quite a few interesting phenomena that result from the fact that satellites rotate while they are orbiting. One reason the received signal from an amateur satellite may exhibit a rapidly repeating fading effect is because **the satellite is spinning**. (E2A10) To mitigate the effects of this fading, you might use a circularly polarized antenna. **A circularly polarized antenna is the** type of antenna that can be used to minimize the effects of spin modulation and Faraday rotation. (E2A11)

Sending up high-altitude balloons with amateur radio equipment has also become a popular part of the hobby. The balloons send telemetry data with various measurements, such as pressure and temperature, and GPS data to track their positions. The position data is sent using **APRS** (Automatic Packet Reporting System), which is the technology used to track, in real time, balloons carrying radio transmitters. (E2A14)

E2B- Television practices: fast scan television standards and techniques; slow scan television standards and techniques

Although we are called "radio" amateurs, we can also transmit and receive television signals. There are several ways that amateurs communicate by television. Perhaps the two most popular ways are standard fast-scan television and slow-scan television (SSTV).

The video standard used by North American Fast Scan ATV stations is called **NTSC**. (E2B16) The NTSC, or National Television Systems Committee, is the body that set standards for the analog television system that was used in the U.S. and many other parts of the world. After nearly 70 years of using the analog NTSC system, U.S. broadcasters switched over to a digital broadcasting system on June 12, 2009.

A fast-scan (NTSC) television frame has **525** horizontal lines (E2B02), and a new frame is transmitted **30** times per second in a fast-scan (NTSC) television system. (E2B01) NTSC systems use an interlaced scanning pattern. An interlaced scanning pattern is generated in a fast-scan (NTSC) television system **by scanning odd numbered lines in one field and even numbered ones in the next**. (E2B03)

In order for the scanning beam to only show the picture, a technique called blanking is used. Blanking in a video signal is **turning off the scanning beam while it is traveling from right to left or from bottom to top**. (E2B04)

NTSC signals are amplitude modulated (AM) signals, but use a technique called vestigial sideband modulation. Vestigial sideband modulation is **amplitude modulation in which one complete sideband and a portion of the other are transmitted**. (E2B06) The reason that NTSC TV uses vestigial modulation is to conserve bandwidth. Even using this technique, an NTSC signal is 6 MHz wide. One advantage of using vestigial sideband for standard fast-scan TV transmissions is that **vestigial sideband reduces bandwidth while allowing for simple video detector circuitry**. (E2B05)

Amateurs can transmit color TV as well as black-and-white TV.

The name of the signal component that carries color information in NTSC video is **chroma**. (E2B07)

There are a number of different ways to transmit audio with an NTSC signal. The following are common methods of transmitting accompanying audio with amateur fast-scan television:

- Frequency-modulated sub-carrier
- A separate VHF or UHF audio link
- Frequency modulation of the video carrier

All of these choices are correct. (E2B08)

Because of the bandwidth requirements, amateurs can only transmit fast-scan TV above 440 MHz. FM ATV transmissions, for example, are likely to be found on **1255 MHz**. (E2B18)

Slow-scan TV (SSTV)

Because SSTV is normally found on the HF bands where bandwidth is at a premium, one special operating frequency restriction imposed on slow scan TV transmissions is that **they are restricted to phone band segments and their bandwidth can be no greater than that of a voice signal of the same modulation type**. (E2B19) The approximate bandwidth of a slow-scan TV signal is, therefore, **3 kHz**. (E2B17)

SSTV images are typically transmitted on the HF bands by **varying tone frequencies representing the video are transmitted using single sideband**. (E2B12) The **tone frequency** of an amateur slow-scan television signal encodes the brightness of the picture. (E2B14)

128 or 256 lines are commonly used in each frame on an amateur slow-scan color television picture. (E2B13) **Specific tone frequencies** signal SSTV receiving equipment to begin a new picture line. (E2B15)

There are a number of different SSTV modes. The function of the Vertical Interval Signaling (VIS) code transmitted as part of an SSTV transmission is **to identify the SSTV mode being used**. (E2B11)

Digital Radio Mondiale is one way to send and receive SSTV signals. **No other hardware is needed**, other than a receiver with SSB capability and a suitable computer, to decode SSTV using Digital Radio Mondiale (DRM). (E2B09) Just like any SSTV transmission, 3 KHz is an acceptable bandwidth for Digital Radio Mondiale (DRM) based voice or SSTV digital transmissions made on the HF amateur bands. (E2B10)

E2C - Operating methods: contest and DX operating; remote operation techniques; Cabrillo format; QSLing; RF network connected systems

Contesting is one of the most popular activities in amateur radio. While the rules differ from contest to contest, in general, the goal is to make as many contacts as possible in a given time period.

To enter a contest and be considered for awards, you must submit a log of your contacts. The contest organizers will check the log to make sure that you actually made the contacts that you claim. To make this easier to do, most contest organizers now request that you send in a digital file that lists your contacts in the Cabrillo format. The Cabrillo format is **a standard for submission of electronic contest logs**. (E2C07)

In contest operating, **operators are permitted to make contacts even if they do not submit a log**. (E2C01) If you do not submit a log, you obviously cannot win a contest, but there are several reasons why you still might choose to participate in a contest. For example, for big DX contests, some amateurs travel to locations where amateur radio operation is infrequent. Making contact with those stations during a contest gives you an opportunity to add countries to your total.

Another reason is that it will give you a good idea of the capabilities of your station. If, for example, during a contest, you need to call repeatedly before a DX station replies, it might mean that you should improve your antenna system.

There are some operating practices that are either prohibited or highly discouraged when operating a contest. On the HF bands, for example, operating on the "WARC bands," is normally prohibited. Therefore, **30 meters** is one band on which amateur radio contesting is generally excluded. (E2C03). The other "WARC bands" are 17 meters and 12 meters.

Another prohibited practice is "self-spotting." Self-spotting is **the generally prohibited practice of posting one's own call sign and frequency on a call sign spotting network**. (E2C02) The reason this is prohibited is that doing so might give you an advantage over other operators.

VHF/UHF contests rarely include FM operation. During a VHF/UHF contest, you would, therefore, expect to find the highest level of activity **in the weak signal segment of the band, with most of the activity near the calling frequency**. (E2C06)

"Working" DX

"Working DX," or contacting stations in far-off places, is one of the most popular amateur radio activities. To be successful at working DX you need to know the protocol or etiquette involved in doing so. For example, **sending your full call sign once or twice** is the way you should generally identify your station when attempting to contact a DX station working a pileup or in a contest. (E2C11)

When many stations want to contact a DX station, it may become almost impossible for the DX station to hear anyone calling him. When this happens, the DX station often listens for calls on another frequency, usually above the frequency on which he is transmitting. We call this "split operation." **All of these choices are correct** as reasons why might a DX station state that they are listening on another frequency (E2C10):

- Because the DX station may be transmitting on a frequency that is prohibited to some responding stations
- To separate the calling stations from the DX station
- To reduce interference, thereby improving operating efficiency

Being aware of propagation conditions can also help you work more DX. For example, one thing that might help to restore contact when DX signals become too weak to copy across an entire HF band a few hours after sunset is to **switch to a lower frequency HF band**. (E2C12)

After you've made contact with a DX station, you may want to receive confirmation of that contact. You'll need confirmation, for example, to qualify for awards, such as Worked All Continents or the DX Century Club. An economical way to do this is to use the QSL bureau. **Contacts between a U.S. station and a non-U.S. station** may be confirmed through the U.S. QSL bureau system. (E2C08)

What the bureau does is group QSL cards to be sent to a particular country and sends hundreds or thousands of them in a single shipment to the QSL bureau in that country. The DX QSL bureau then sorts the cards and sends them to individual amateurs. This makes sending and receiving QSL cards from DX station much cheaper, but it may take a year or more to receive a reply from a DX station.

Some DX stations have QSL managers handle the sometimes arduous task of QSLing for them. The function of a DX QSL Manager is **to handle the receiving and sending of confirmation cards for a DX station**. (E2C05) The nice thing about sending QSL cards to and receiving QSL cards from a QSL manager is that the process is often much faster than going through a bureau.

Mesh networks and remote operation

Because the amateur radio band at 2.4 GHZ overlaps with some WiFi channels, some amateurs are using those frequencies to set up digital networks called mesh networks. The type of transmission most often used for a ham radio mesh network is **spread spectrum in the 2.4 GHz band**. (E2C04) **A standard wireless router running custom software** is commonly used to implement a ham radio mesh network. (E2C09)

Connecting to amateur radio stations over the Internet has made remote operation easier than ever before. A frequently asked question about remote operation is whether or not a special indicator is required when operating a remote station. **No additional indicator is required** to be used by U.S.-licensed operators when operating a station via remote control where the transmitter is located in the U.S. (E2C13)

E2D - Operating methods: VHF and UHF digital modes and procedures; APRS; EME procedures, meteor scatter procedures

One of the most commonly misunderstood concepts in digital communications is the baud. A baud is not equal to a bit per second, except for very simple systems. Rather, the definition of baud is the number of data symbols transmitted per second, and a data symbol may represent multiple bits.

While modern Internet digital communication techniques can send and receive digital data at megabit per second (Mbps) speeds, digital communications over amateur radio links is much slower. Under clear communications conditions, **300-baud packet** is the digital communication mode that has the fastest data throughput. (E2D09)

JT65

In the past ten years or so, the number of digital modes has just exploded. JT65 is one example. The type of modulation used for JT65 contacts is **multi-tone AFSK**. (E2D13) One advantage of using JT65 coding is **the ability to decode signals which have a very low signal to noise ratio**. (E2D14)

JT65 is a digital mode especially useful for EME communications. (E2D03) JT65 improves EME communications because **it can decode signals many dB below the noise floor using FEC**.(E2D12) One of the reasons that JT65 is such an effective method of establishing EME contacts is because it uses **time synchronous transmissions alternately from each station**. (E2D06) JT65 software organizes the timing of contacts by **alternating transmissions at 1 minute intervals**. (E2E03)

APRS

One of the most popular digital modes is the Automatic Packet Reporting System, or APRS. Most APRS operation takes place on the 2 m band around 144.39 MHz.

AX.25 is the digital protocol used by APRS. (E2D07) AX.25 is more commonly known as packet radio. **Unnumbered Information** is the type of packet frame used to transmit APRS beacon data. (E2D08)

APRS stations can be used to help support a public service communications activity. **An APRS station with a GPS unit can automatically transmit information to show a mobile station's position during the event.** (E2D10) **Latitude and longitude** are used by the APRS network to communicate your location. (E2D11)

Meteor scatter

Digital modes can also be used to make meteor scatter contacts. **FSK441** is a digital mode especially designed for use for meteor scatter signals. (E2D01) **All of these choices are correct** when talking about good techniques for making meteor scatter contacts: (E2D02)

- 15 second timed transmission sequences with stations alternating based on location
- Use of high speed CW or digital modes
- Short transmission with rapidly repeated call signs and signal reports

Satellite digital communications

Amateurs that enjoy satellite communications also use digital modes. For example, **store-and-forward** is a technique normally used by low Earth orbiting digital satellites to relay messages around the world. (E2D05) The purpose of digital store-and-forward functions on an Amateur Radio satellite is **to store digital messages in the satellite for later download by other stations.** (E2D04)

E2E - Operating methods: operating HF digital modes

Perhaps the most popular digital mode these days is PSK31. PSK stands for "phase shift keying." One of its main advantages is that it had a very narrow bandwidth—only 31 Hz. In fact, **PSK31** is the digital communications mode that has the narrowest bandwidth. (E2E10)

One of the reasons that PSK31 has such a narrow bandwidth is that it uses variable length coding. That is to say, characters have different numbers of bits, depending on how frequently they appear in normal text. **PSK31** is an HF digital mode that uses variable-length coding for bandwidth efficiency. (E2E09)

Another type of modulation commonly used on the HF bands is frequency-shift keying, or FSK. RTTY, for example uses FSK modulation. **FSK** is a type of modulation that is common for data emissions below 30 MHz. (E2E01) Another digital mode that uses FSK modulation is MFSK16. The typical bandwidth of a properly modulated MFSK16 signal is **316 Hz.** (E2E07)

Amateur transceivers use two different methods to modulate a signal using FSK: direct FSK and audio FSK. The difference between direct FSK and audio FSK is that **direct FSK applies the data signal to the transmitter VFO.** (E2E11) When using audio FSK, audio, typically from a computer sound card, is used to shift the frequency of the transmitted signal.

To tune an FSK signal, one often uses a crossed-ellipse display. You have properly tuned a signal when one of the ellipses is as vertical as possible, and the other is as horizontal as possible. When one of the ellipses in an FSK crossed-ellipse display suddenly disappears, **selective fading has occurred.** (E2E04)

PACTOR is another digital mode that uses FSK. It also uses the ARQ protocol to detect errors. Because of this, **PACTOR** is an HF digital mode that can be used to transfer binary files. (E2E08)

Another way to detect and correct errors in a data transmission is forward error correction. The letters FEC mean **Forward Error Correction** as they relate to digital operation. (E2E02)

No matter what type of modulation you use, data transmission over an HF radio link is very slow. **300 baud** is the most common data rate used for HF packet communications. (E2E06) In fact, due to bandwidth limitations, 300 baud is the maximum symbol rate.

Some HF digital modes operate automatically, that is to say the software running these digital modes automatically initiate and maintain the connection. One technique for doing this is called Automatic Link Enable (ALE). Stations using the Automatic Link Enable (ALE) protocol use **automatic** control. (E2E12)

Winlink is one of the digital modes that uses ALE. **Winlink** is, therefore, one digital mode that does not support keyboard-to-keyboard operation. E2E05)

Of course, as we all know, when using HF links, any number of things can go wrong. **All of these choices are correct** when considering the possible reasons that attempts to initiate contact with a digital station on a clear frequency are unsuccessful: (E2E13)

- Your transmit frequency is incorrect
- The protocol version you are using is not the supported by the digital station
- Another station you are unable to hear is using the frequency

E0: SAFETY

E0A Safety: amateur radio safety practices; RF radiation hazards; hazardous materials; grounding

No matter what amateur radio activities you engage in, I hope that you will engage in them safely. Every year, we lose amateur radio operators because of injuries they sustained while putting up antennas or doing things that could be dangerous. We don't want to lose you.

Perhaps the most common danger is from lightning strikes. To mitigate the danger of a lightning strike, you should use properly grounded lighting arrestors. The primary function of an external earth connection or ground rod is **lightning protection**. (E0A01)

RF exposure is another hazard. One of the ways that RF exposure can be hazardous is by causing human tissue to heat up. The amount of heating is proportional to the specific absorption rate (SAR). SAR measures **the rate at which RF energy is absorbed by the body**. (E0A08)

In general, the SAR increases as the frequency increases. Think microwave ovens. They heat food because water in the food absorbs microwave radiation. The maximum permissible exposure (MPE) is the level at which harmful biological effects can occur. Several organizations, including the National Council on Radiation Protection and Measurements (NCRP) and the Institute of Electrical and Electronics Engineers (IEEE) have provided the data used by the FCC to set MPEs.

Localized heating of the body from RF exposure in excess of the MPE limits is an injury that can result from using high-power UHF or microwave transmitters. (E0A11) One of the potential hazards of using microwaves in the amateur radio bands is that **the high gain antennas commonly used can result in high exposure levels**. (E0A05)

The FCC, as you might expect, has a lot to say about RF exposure. They have set limits on the field strengths that humans may be exposed to. These limits are called maximum permissible exposure, or MPE.

The MPEs for the electric field and magnetic field of an electromagnetic wave differ. **All of these choices are correct** as to why there are separate electric (E) and magnetic (H) field MPE limits (E0A06):

- The body reacts to electromagnetic radiation from both the E and H fields
- Ground reflections and scattering make the field impedance vary with location
- E field and H field radiation intensity peaks can occur at different locations

To make sure that your transmissions do not expose you or others to field strengths above the MPE limits, you could measure the absolute field strengths. Unfortunately, this is not easy to do. The equipment used to measure field strength is very expensive and difficult to use. An alternative is to use software that calculates field strength. **Using an antenna modeling program to calculate field strength at accessible locations** would be a practical way to estimate whether the RF fields produced by an amateur radio station are within permissible MPE limits. (E0A03)

Remember to include your neighbors when evaluating RF exposure levels. In some cases, your antennas may actually be closer to your neighbors' houses than they are to your house. When evaluating RF exposure levels from your station at a neighbor's home, you must

make sure signals from your station are less than the uncontrolled MPE limits. (E0A02)

Typically, amateur repeater stations are located in places where there are transmitters for other radio services, such as cell phone and pager services. These sites should be regularly evaluated so that RF field strengths don't exceed the MPE limits. When evaluating a site with multiple transmitters operating at the same time, the operators and licensees of **each transmitter that produces 5 percent or more of its MPE exposure limit at accessible locations** are responsible for mitigating over-exposure situations. (E0A04)

Lightning and RF exposure are not the only dangers posed by an amateur radio station. For example, in emergency situations, you may want to use a gasoline-powered generator. One of the dangers posed by a gas-powered generator is that its exhaust contains carbon monoxide. Dangerous levels of carbon monoxide from an emergency generator can be detected **only with a carbon monoxide detector**. (E0A07)

Some of the materials used in electronics pose a danger to amateur radio operators. They are used because they have some desirable electrical property, but may be dangerous if used improperly. For example, **beryllium oxide** is an insulating material commonly used as a thermal conductor for some types of electronic devices that is extremely toxic if broken or crushed and the particles are accidentally inhaled. (E0A09) **Polychlorinated biphenyls**, or PCBs, are materials found in some electronic components, such as high-voltage capacitors and transformers, that is considered toxic. (E0A10)

E1: COMMISSION'S RULES

E1A Operating Standards: frequency privileges; emission standards; automatic message forwarding; frequency sharing; stations aboard ships or aircraft

When using a transceiver that displays the carrier frequency of phone signals, the highest frequency at which a properly adjusted USB emission will be totally within the band is **3 kHz below the upper band edge**. (E1A01) So, with your transceiver displaying the carrier frequency of phone signals, you hear a DX station's CQ on 14.349 MHz USB. Is it legal to return the call using upper sideband on the same frequency? **No, the sidebands will extend beyond the band edge.** (E1A03)

The reason for this is that a USB signal extends from the carrier frequency, which is the frequency that the transceiver is displaying, up 3 kHz. When you set the transceiver to 14.349 kHz, the upper sideband will extend up to 14.352 MHz, and because the amateur radio band stops at 14.350 MHz, some of the transmission will fall outside the band.

A similar thing happens, but in reverse, when you operate lower sideband, or LSB. When using a transceiver that displays the carrier frequency of phone signals, the lowest frequency at which a properly adjusted LSB emission will be totally within the band is **3 kHz above the lower band edge**. (E1A02) With your transceiver displaying the carrier frequency of phone signals, you hear a DX station calling CQ on 3.601 MHz LSB. Is it legal to return the call using lower sideband on the same frequency? **No, the sideband will extend beyond the edge of the phone band segment**. (E1A04)

The lower sideband extends from the carrier frequency down 3 kHz. So, when your transceiver is set to 3.601 MHz, your signal will extend down to 3.598 MHz, which is outside the phone band.

This is also a consideration when operating CW because a CW signal occupies a finite bandwidth. With your transceiver displaying the carrier frequency of CW signals, if you hear a DX station's CQ on 3.500 MHz, it is not legal to return the call using CW on the same frequency because **one of the sidebands of the CW signal will be out of the band**. (E1A12)

60 m band

The 60 m band is one of the oddest amateur radio bands. One of the reasons for this is that the **60 meter band** is the only amateur band where transmission on specific channels rather than a range of frequencies is permitted. (E1A07) Also, the carrier frequency of a CW signal that complies with FCC rules for 60 meter operation must be set **at the center frequency of the channel,** (E1A06) and the maximum bandwidth for a data emission on 60m is **2.8 kHz**. (E1A14)

The rules for power output are also a bit arcane. The maximum power output permitted on the 60 meter band is **100 watts PEP effective radiated power relative to the gain of a half-wave dipole**. (E1A05) The rules are written this way to minimize interference between amateur radio operators, who are secondary users of this band, and the primary users, which are primarily government radio stations.

Winlink

Some amateur radio systems automatically forward messages for other amateur radio stations. Winlink is one such system. There is always a question of who is responsible when an automatically-controlled station forwards a message that violates FCC rules.

If a station in a message forwarding system inadvertently forwards a message that is in violation of FCC rules, **the control operator of the originating station** is primarily accountable for the rules violation, (E1A08) This is very similar to the situation where a repeater is used to send messages that violate FCC rules.

The first action you should take if your digital message forwarding station inadvertently forwards a communication that violates FCC rules is to **discontinue forwarding the communication as soon as you become aware of it**. (E1A09) This is also similar to what a repeater control operator should do if a repeater user is violating FCC rules.

Operating aboard a ship or airplane

Operating an amateur radio station aboard a ship or an airplane can be a lot of fun, but there are some rules that govern this operation. For example, if an amateur station is installed aboard a ship or aircraft, **its operation must be approved by the master of the ship or the pilot in command of the aircraft** before the station is operated. (E1A10) **Any FCC-issued amateur license** is required when operating an amateur station aboard a U.S.-registered vessel in international waters. (E1A11)

Even when operating from a ship, there must be a control operator. **Any person holding an FCC-issued amateur license or who is authorized for alien reciprocal operation** must be in physical control of the station apparatus of an amateur station aboard any vessel or craft that is documented or registered in the United States. (E1A13)

E1B - Station restrictions and special operations: restrictions on station location; general operating restrictions, spurious emissions, control operator reimbursement; antenna structure restrictions; RACES operations; National Quiet Zone

Part 97 places many different restrictions on how amateurs can use their stations and specifies technical standards that amateur radio station must meet. For example, some rules set standards for spurious emissions. A spurious emission is **an emission outside its necessary bandwidth that can be reduced or eliminated without affecting the information transmitted.** (E1B01) The rules also state that permitted mean power of any spurious emission relative to the mean power of the fundamental emission from a station transmitter or external RF amplifier must be **at least 43 dB below** for transmitters or amplifiers installed after January 1, 2003, and transmitting on a frequency below 30 MHz. (E1B11)

There are also restrictions on erecting antennas. One factor that might cause the physical location of an amateur station apparatus or antenna structure to be restricted is if **the location is of environmental importance or significant in American history, architecture, or culture.** (E1B02) If you are installing an amateur station antenna at a site at or near a public use airport, **you may have to notify the Federal Aviation Administration and register it with the FCC as required by Part 17 of FCC rules.** (E1B06)

Because RACES operation is quasi-governmental, there are some rules about RACES operations. **Any FCC-licensed amateur station certified by the responsible civil defense organization for the area served** may be operated in RACES. (E1B09) **All amateur service frequencies authorized to the control operator** are authorized to an amateur station participating in RACES. (E1B10)

Finally, there are some questions about random rules in this section:

- The distance at which an amateur station must protect an FCC monitoring facility from harmful interference is **1 mile.** (E1B03)

- **An Environmental Assessment must be submitted to the FCC** must be done before placing an amateur station within an officially designated wilderness area or wildlife preserve, or an area listed in the National Register of Historical Places. (E1B04)
- The National Quiet Zone is **an area surrounding the National Radio Astronomy Observatory.** (E1B05) The NRAO is located in Green Bank, West Virginia.
- **The amateur station must avoid transmitting during certain hours on frequencies that cause the interference** if its signal causes interference to domestic broadcast reception, assuming that the receiver(s) involved are of good engineering design. (E1B08)
- The highest modulation index permitted at the highest modulation frequency for angle modulation is **1.0.** (E1B07)

E1C - Definitions and restrictions pertaining to local, automatic and remote control operation; control operator responsibilities for remote and automatically controlled stations; IARP and CEPT licenses; third party communications over automatically controlled stations

An important concept in the rules governing amateur radio is the concept of station control and the control operator. The control operator is the licensed radio amateur who is responsible for the transmissions of a station, and the location of that operator is called the control point. There are three ways that a control operator can control a station: local control, remote control, or automatic control.

Local control means **direct manipulation of the transmitter by a control operator**. (E1C07) So, when you were sitting in front of your radio, you are using local control.

A remotely controlled station is **a station controlled indirectly through a control link**. (E1C01) When an amateur station is being remotely controlled, **a control operator must be present at the control point**. (E1C06) This is, of course, true for local control as well. **3 minutes** is the maximum permissible duration of a remotely controlled station's transmissions if its control link malfunctions. (E1C08)

Automatic control of a station means **the use of devices and procedures for control so that the control operator does not have to be present at a control point**. (E1C02) The control operator responsibilities of a station under automatic control differs from one under local control. **Under automatic control the control operator is not required to be present at the control point.** (E1C03)

Most repeaters are operated with automatic control. **Only auxiliary, repeater or space stations** are the types of amateur stations that may automatically retransmit the radio signals of other amateur stations. (E1C10) **29.500 - 29.700 MHz** is the frequency band available for an automatically-controlled repeater operating below 30 MHz. (E1C09) No repeaters are allowed on any other HF band. An automatically controlled station may **never** originate third party communications. (E1C05)

IARP and CEPT licenses, third-party traffic

An IARP is **an international amateur radio permit that allows U.S. amateurs to operate in certain countries of the Americas**. (E1C04) Countries that accept an IARP include Argentina, Brazil, Canada, El Salvador, Panama, Paraguay, Peru, Trinidad and Tobago, United States of America, Uruguay, and Venezuela. In the U.S., IARPs are issued by the ARRL.

The CEPT agreement allows an FCC-licensed U.S. citizen to operate in many European countries, and alien amateurs from many European countries to operate in the U.S. (E1C11) **You must bring a copy of FCC Public Notice DA 11-221** to operate in accordance with CEPT rules in foreign countries where permitted. (E1C13) There are 40 European countries that allow you to operate under the CEPT agreement.

Apart from these two agreements, amateurs with Canadian licenses are allowed to operate in U.S. without any special license or permit. The privileges authorized in the U.S. to persons holding an amateur service license granted by the Government of Canada include **the operating terms and conditions of the Canadian amateur service license, not to exceed U.S. Extra Class privileges**. (E1F02)

Remember that when operating in a foreign country or even here in the U.S., **communications incidental to the purpose of the amateur service and remarks of a personal nature** are the only types of communications may be transmitted to amateur stations in foreign countries. (E1C12)

E1D - Amateur satellites: definitions and purpose; license requirements for space stations; available frequencies and bands; telecommand and telemetry operations; restrictions, and special provisions; notification requirements

The amateur satellite service is **a radio communications service using amateur radio stations on satellites**. (E1D02) In the amateur satellite service, the satellites are called space stations and are remotely controlled by telecommands.

Only 40m, 20m, 17m, 15m, 12m and 10m are the amateur service HF bands have frequencies authorized to space stations. (E1D07) **2 meters** is the only VHF amateur service band that has frequencies available for space stations. (E1D08) **70 cm and 13 cm** are the UHF amateur service bands that have frequencies available for a space station. (E1D09)

One special provision that a space station must incorporate in order to comply with space station requirements is that **the space station must be capable of terminating transmissions by telecommand when directed by the FCC.** (E1D06) A telecommand station in the amateur satellite service is **an amateur station that transmits communications to initiate, modify or terminate functions of a space station.** (E1D03)

An amateur station eligible to be a telecommand station is **any amateur station so designated by the space station licensee, subject to the privileges of the class of operator license held by the control operator.** (E1D10) **Licensees of any class with appropriate operator privileges** are authorized to be the control operator of a space station. (E1D05)

Another important concept in the amateur satellite service is the Earth station. An Earth station in the amateur satellite service is **an amateur station within 50 km of the Earth's surface intended for communications with amateur stations by means of objects in space.** (E1D04) **Any amateur station, subject to the privileges of the class of operator license held by the control operator** is eligible to operate as an Earth station. (E1D11)

To obtain information about the operation of the space station itself, many space stations send telemetry. Telemetry is defined as **one-way transmission of measurements at a distance from the measuring instrument.** (E1D01)

E1E - Volunteer examiner program: definitions; qualifications; preparation and administration of exams; accreditation; question pools; documentation requirements

The Volunteer Examiner program started in the early 1980s, and has been a boon for amateur radio. Exam sessions are now more accessible than when tests were given by the FCC, meaning that it is much easier to obtain an amateur radio license, and that more people can now enjoy our hobby.

As the name implies, volunteer examiners (VEs) are volunteers. They may not accept any payment for administering tests. They may, however, be reimbursed for some expenses. **Preparing, processing, administering and coordinating an examination for an amateur radio license** are the types of out-of-pocket expenses that Part 97 rules state that VEs and VECs may be reimbursed. (E1E14)

The organizations that are responsible for accrediting and administering the exams are called Volunteer Examiner Coordinators (VECs). A Volunteer Examiner Coordinator is **an organization that has entered into an agreement with the FCC to coordinate amateur operator license examinations**. (E1E03) There are currently 14 VECs in the U.S. **The procedure by which a VEC confirms that the VE applicant meets FCC requirements to serve as an examiner** is the phrase that describes the Volunteer Examiner accreditation process. (E1E04)

The National Conference of Volunteer Examiner Coordinators (NCVEC) is a group made up from representatives of the 14 VECs. The NCVEC is responsible for maintaining the question pools for the three examinations. The questions for all written US amateur license examinations are listed **in a question pool maintained by all the VECs**. (E1E02)

The rules and procedures for administering the tests are written so that everything is on the up and up. For example, **3** is the minimum number of qualified VEs required to administer an Element 4 amateur operator license examination. (E1E01) **Each administering VE** is responsible for the proper conduct and necessary supervision during an amateur operator license examination session. (E1E06) Having three VEs present at a test session, and making them all responsible for how they conduct the test session, leaves very little room for cheating.

VEs are not to show any favoritism. To minimize the chance of this happening, a VE may not administer an examination to **relatives of the VE as listed in the FCC rules**. (E1E08)

The penalty for a VE who fraudulently administers or certifies an examination can be **revocation of the VE's amateur station license grant and the suspension of the VE's amateur operator license grant**. (E1E09)

Before administering a test, the VEs instruct the candidates of the rules. For example, the candidates are not allowed to consult any books during the test. They may use a calculator, but only if they can demonstrate to a VE that all of the calculator's memories have been cleared. If a candidate fails to comply with the examiner's instructions during an amateur operator license examination, a VE should **immediately terminate the candidate's examination**. (E1E07)

After the test, three VEs must correct each test sheet. This minimizes the chance for making a scoring mistake. On amateur operator license examinations, there is a **minimum passing score of 74%**. (E1E05) If an examinee scores a passing grade on all examination elements needed for an upgrade or new license, **three VEs must certify that the examinee is qualified for the license grant and that they have complied with the administering VE requirements**. (E1E11)

After the administration of a successful examination for an amateur operator license, the VEs **must submit the application document to the coordinating VEC according to the coordinating VEC instructions**. (E1E10) If the examinee does not pass the exam, the VE team must **return the application document to the examinee**. (E1E12)

A recent rules change allows VEs to administer exams remotely. This allows applicants living in remote locations to more easily take an amateur radio license examination. An acceptable method for monitoring the applicants if a VEC opts to conduct an exam session remotely is to **use a real-time video link and the Internet to connect the exam session to the observing VEs.** (E1E13)

E1F - Miscellaneous rules: external RF power amplifiers; business communications; compensated communications; spread spectrum; auxiliary stations; reciprocal operating privileges; special temporary authority

As the name of this section implies, it contains a hodgepodge of questions covering sometimes obscure rules. About the only way to get these right is to memorize the answers.

The use of spread-spectrum techniques is a topic that comes up from time to time. Many amateurs feel that the rules are too restrictive. For example, **10 W** is the maximum transmitter power for an amateur station transmitting spread spectrum communications (E1F10), and **only on amateur frequencies above 222 MHz** are spread spectrum transmissions permitted. (E1F01)

All of these choices are correct when talking about the conditions that apply when transmitting spread spectrum emission: (E1F09)

- A station transmitting SS emission must not cause harmful interference to other stations employing other authorized emissions.
- The transmitting station must be in an area regulated by the FCC or in a country that permits SS emissions.
- The transmission must not be used to obscure the meaning of any communication.

External RF power amplifiers

The rules governing the use of external amplifiers is also somewhat controversial. A dealer may sell an external RF power amplifier capable of operation below 144 MHz if it has not been granted FCC certification if **it was purchased in used condition from an amateur operator and is sold to another amateur operator for use at that operator's station.** (E1F03) One of the standards that must be met by an external RF power amplifier if it is to qualify for a grant of FCC certification is that it **must satisfy the FCC's spurious emission standards when operated at the lesser of 1500 watts, or its full output power.** (E1F11)

There are regulations that protects Canadian Land/Mobile operations near the US/Canadian border from interference. Amateur stations may not transmit in the **420 - 430 MHz** frequency segment if they are located in the contiguous 48 states and north of Line A. (E1F05) **A line roughly parallel to and south of the US-Canadian border** describes "Line A." (E1F04) There is a corresponding "Line B" parallel to and north of the U.S./Canadian border.

Compensated communications

As you might expect, there are some questions about not making any money from operating an amateur radio station. **Communications transmitted for hire or material compensation, except as otherwise provided in the rules** are prohibited. (E1F08) An amateur station may send a message to a business only **when neither the amateur nor his or her employer has a pecuniary interest in the communications**. (E1F07)

This next question is a bit of a trick question. 97.201 states that **only Technician, General, Advanced or Amateur Extra Class operators** may be the control operator of an auxiliary station. (E1F12) It's a trick question because there are also holders of Novice Class licenses, even though no new Novice licenses have been issued for many years.

Special temporary authority

Some amateurs are granted special privileges called special temporary authority. The FCC issues a Special Temporary Authority (STA) to an amateur station **to provide for experimental amateur communications**. (E1F06)

ABOUT THE AUTHOR

I have been a ham radio operator since 1971 and a radio enthusiast as long as I can remember. In addition to being an active CW operator on the HF bands:

- I blog about amateur radio at KB6NU.Com, one of the leading amateur radio blogs on the Internet.
- I am the author of the *No-Nonsense Technician Class License Study Guide* and the *No-Nonsense General Class License Study Guide*. These publications are available in PDF format, in Kindle and Nook e-book formats, and in print. See http://www.kb6nu.com/study-guides for more information.
- I am the author of *The CW Geek's Guide to Having Fun with Morse Code*, a book for those who are interested in the art of operating CW. You can find it on my website or on Amazon or Barnes&Noble. Like my other books, it's available as an e-book or in print.
- I am the author of *21 Things to Do With your Amateur Radio License*, a book for those who have been recently licensed or just getting back into the hobby. You can find it on my website, or on Amazon or Barnes&Noble. Like my other books, it's available as an e-book or in print.
- I send out a monthly column to nearly 400 amateur radio clubs in North America for publication in their newsletters.
- I am the station manager for WA2HOM (http://www.wa2hom.org), the amateur radio station at the Ann Arbor Hands-On Museum (http://www.aahom.org).

- I teach amateur radio classes around the state of Michigan.
- I serve as the ARRL Michigan Section Training Manager and conduct amateur radio leadership workshops for amateur radio club leaders in Michigan.

You can contact me by sending e-mail to cwgeek@kb6nu.com. If you have comments or questions about any of the stuff in this book, I hope you will do so.

73!

Dan, KB6NU

ALSO BY KB6NU

No-Nonsense Technician Class License Study Guide
(for tests given between July 2014 and June 2018)
Thousands of amateur radio operators have used the No-Nonsense study guides to get into amateur radio. You can, too. You will learn everything you need to know to get your Technician Class amateur radio license. Written in a simple, easy-to-understand style, this study guide will get you on the air in no time.

No-Nonsense General Class License Study Guide
(for tests given between July 2015 and June 2019)
Written in a simple, easy-to-understand style, this study guide will help you upgrade to General Class in no time. This study guide covers every single question that you'll find on the test.

The CW Geek's Guide to Having Fun with Morse Code
The *CW Geek's Guide to Having Fun with Morse Code* is full of practical information that will help ham radio operators have fun learning and using Morse Code. Chapters include:
- Learning the Code. This chapter gives advice on how to learn the code, including recommendations for programs and websites that you can use for free.
- Getting on the Air. This chapter describes, in my "no nonsense" style how to tune in CW signals, how to make contact, and then what to do once you have made contact.
- Choosing a Key. This chapter describes the different types of keys available and how to choose the one that's right for you. Keyers. This chapter describes the different types of keyers and how to connect them to your radio.
- References and Resources. This section includes information on Q-signals, RST signal reporting, abbreviations, CW clubs, and other resources that will be useful for amateur radio

operators.

21 Things to Do After You Get Your Amateur Radio License

Congratulations! You passed the test and have an amateur radio license. Now what? *21 Things to Do After You Get Your Amateur Radio License*, tells you what. The 21 different activities in the book will not only suggest things you can do with your ham license, but more importantly, how to have fun with amateur radio. You'll discover:

- How and why to join a club
- What things to think about before you buy a radio
- How to set up a "shack"
- Why you should build a kit or an antenna
- How to learn Morse Code
- How to participate in public-service and emergency communications events
- Plus much, much, more...

E-books versions can be purchased from KB6NU.Com. Print versions are available from Amazon.

Made in the USA
Monee, IL
27 September 2021

Made in the USA
San Bernardino, CA
18 February 2017